MANDATE FOR CHANGE:
Dynamics of Electoral Politics in Manipur

MANDATE FOR CHANGE:
Dynamics of Electoral Politics in Manipur

Abu Nasar Saied Ahmed
Elizabeth Devi Kh
Maqbul Ali
Ratna Bhuyan

OMEO KUMAR DAS INSTITUTE OF SOCIAL CHANGE AND DEVELOPMENT
&

AKANSHA PUBLISHING HOUSE
NEW DELHI-110002 (INDIA)

AKANSHA PUBLISHING HOUSE
4649-B/21, Ansari Road
Darya Ganj, New Delhi - 110 002
Ph.: 23263193 / 9811582579 / 09435116718
Fax: 011-23263193
Email: ektabooks@yahoo.com
www.akanshapublishinghouse.com

Mandate for Change: Dynamics of Electoral Politics in Manipur

First Published 2009
ISBN 978-81-8370-173-0

PRINTED IN INDIA

Published by Akansha Publishing House, New Delhi, and Printed at Aryan Enterprises, Delhi.

To

Professor Lokendra Arambam

Scholar, Artist and Humanist

CONTENTS

PREFACE

Manipur is one of the most fascinating states of Indian Union. Its enchanting hills, dancing rivers and rivulets, its blue water lake, its various art forms such as melodious music, thrilling dances, captive theatres, its sporting personality as reflected through the outstanding performance of the sports personalities, its hardworking women and their colourful dresses, its people living in hills and plains and their magnificent varied cultures and traditions always transcend to charm others. That is why Pandit Jawaharlal Nehru once said, "Manipur is a jewel on the crown".

Yet, Manipur is one of the most unfortunate states in the country, afflicted by underdevelopment, instability and insurgency. For 40 years, the state suffered grievously because of acute form of political instability caused by frequent change of governments. It is argued that insurgency in the state is to be attributed to political instability together with the problems of underdevelopment. Four decades is a quite long period of time for insurgency to grow to a formidable extent. Despite the fact that the electorate come out in a massive way to cast vote, their fractured verdict leads to temporary arrangement of running the state government on ad hoc basis. Therefore, not a single ministry could complete its five-year term during the period from 1967 to 2002. The elections held in 2002, too, did not give a decisive mandate; yet, the ministry could somehow managed to complete its tenure. The elections of 2007 were epoch making. For the first time, the electorate gave a decisive verdict in favour of political stability as also on certain vital issues concerning the future of the state.

That is why the Assembly elections in Manipur became important not only for the political practitioners, the policy makers, the media but also for the academia, in and outside the state. The present study was driven by the interest generated by the political environment, the issues and campaign trails and the election results. The study has been based on the data available in various sources. The technique of survey research was not used, because of its inherent problems in accuracy, compounded by the difficulties of the ground realities in Manipur where many places remain inaccessible owing to geographic location and insurgency related problems. The hard election data, the issues focused in the manifestoes, the issues figured in the campaign, the very nature of campaign launched by the political parties and the results of the elections vouchsafes for a lot. Interactive engagement with a number of persons associated with the world of academics and the media, and candidates individually, provided many clues to understand the dynamics of the last elections.

As already stated, the present work is not an election survey. It is essentially based on secondary sources of data, complemented with government publications, media highlights and news, and interface with scholars, political leaders, journalists and common citizens. It tries to understand the political climate in which the 9th Assembly elections were held, the nature of alliances that political parties forged before the elections, the issues that figured in the manifestoes of various contesting parties, the nature of the campaign, and above all the people's verdict. It also spells out the message that the electorate wanted to convey to the nation and the decision-makers.

It goes without saying that a number of persons extended enormous help at different stages of the study. One of them, a noble soul who stands anonymous extended great help during the initial stage of the study. In Manipur, we interacted with a good number of persons (some of them desired to remain unnamed), sought their assistance to locate data and interviewed some of the political actors who mattered substantially. All of them extended immense and warm cooperation. To mention some of them with a note of thanks and gratitude, is a pleasant task: they are Gangmumei Kamei, former Professor and Dean of Social Sciences, Lokendra Arambam, former Professor of History, Bimola Devi, Ibo Singh, Professors at Manipur University, Balboo Loitongbam, Executive Director, Human Rights Alert, Dr. Nara Singh, a CPI leader and ex-MLA, Danny Shaiza and R.K. Anand, both Members of Manipur Legislative Assembly, Saroj Kumar Sharma of *Times of India* and Pradip Phanjoubam, Editor of *Imphal Free Press*, and a host of common citizens, for giving us enough time to discuss in depth on the political processes in Manipur. Anuradha Dutta, Professor of Peace Studies at OKDISCD, gave us a lot of clues, to understand politics in a conflict-ridden society like that of Manipur. Indranee Dutta, Director, OKSISCD, provided infrastructural facilities to complete the study. We must thank Rustam Ali for his technical assistance.

The 2007 elections have ushered in a new perspective in the political process in Manipur. Our study should not go in vain as it has provided an academic outline to understand the dynamics that have far-reaching implications.

Abu Nasar Saied Ahmed
Elizabeth Devi Kh
Maqbul Ali
Ratna Bhuyan

September, 2008

LIST OF TABLES

ABBREVIATIONS

AD	Anno Domini
AFSPA	Armed Forces (Special Powers) Act, 1958
AICC	All India Congress Committee
AIDS	Acquired Immune Deficiency Syndrome
AMADA	All Manipur Anti-Drug Association
BJP	Bharatiya Janata Party
BJS	Bharatiya Jan Sangh
BPL	Below Poverty Level
CMIE	Centre for Monitoring Indian Economy
CONSCOM	Consolidation Committee of Manipur
CPI	Communist Party of India
CPI (M)	Communist Party of India (Marxist)
DRPP	Democratic Revolutionary People's Party
ECI	Election Commission of India
FPM	Federal Party of Manipur
GDP	Gross Domestic Product
HIV	Human Immuno deficiency Virus
HPC-D	Hmar People's Convention-Democratic
IIM	Indian Institute of Management

IIT	Indian Institute of Technology
ILF-K	Islamic Liberation Front-Kanglei
IND	Independent
INF	Islamic National Front
KCP	Kangleipak Communist Party
KNA	Kuki National Army/Kuki National Assembly
KNF	Kuki National Front
KNO	Kuki National Organization
KSO	Kuki Student Organization
KYKL	Kanglei Yawol Kanna Lup
LS	Lok Shakti
MDPP	Manipur Democratic People's Party
MHU	Manipur Hill Union
MHPC	Manipur Hill People's Council
MNDP	Manipur National Democratic Party
MPCC	Manipur Pradesh Congress Committee
MPP	Manipur People's Party
MSCP	Manipur State Congress Party
MST	Manipur State Transport
NEMF	North East Minority Front
NLCPR	Non-lapsable Control Pool of Resources
NPP	National People's Party
NREGA	National Rural Employment Guarantee Act
NSA	National Security Act
NSCN(IM)	National Socialist Council of Nagalim (Isak-Muivah)

NSCN (K)	National Socialist Council of Nagalim (Khaplang)
OBC	Other Backward Castes
OKDISCD	Omeo Kumar Das Institute of Social Change and Development
PDA	Progressive Democratic Alliance
PLA	People's Liberation Army
PREPAK	People's Revolutionary Party of Kangleipak
PSP	Praja Socialist Party
PULF	People's United Liberation Front
RGGVY	Rajiv Gandhi Grameen Vidyutikaran Yojna
RGM	'Revolutionary Government of Manipur
RJD	Rashtriya Janata Dal
RPF	Revolutionary People's Front
SAP	Samata Party
SEZ	Special Economic Zone
SP	Samajwadi Party
SPF	Secular Progressive Front
SSP	Sanghata Socialist Party
UKLF	United Kuki Liberation Front
ULP	United Legislative Party
UNC	United Naga Council
UNDF	United Naga Democratic Front
UNLF	United National Liberation Front
UPA	United Progressive Alliance
ZRA	Zomi Revolutionary Army
ZRO	Zomi Reunification Organization

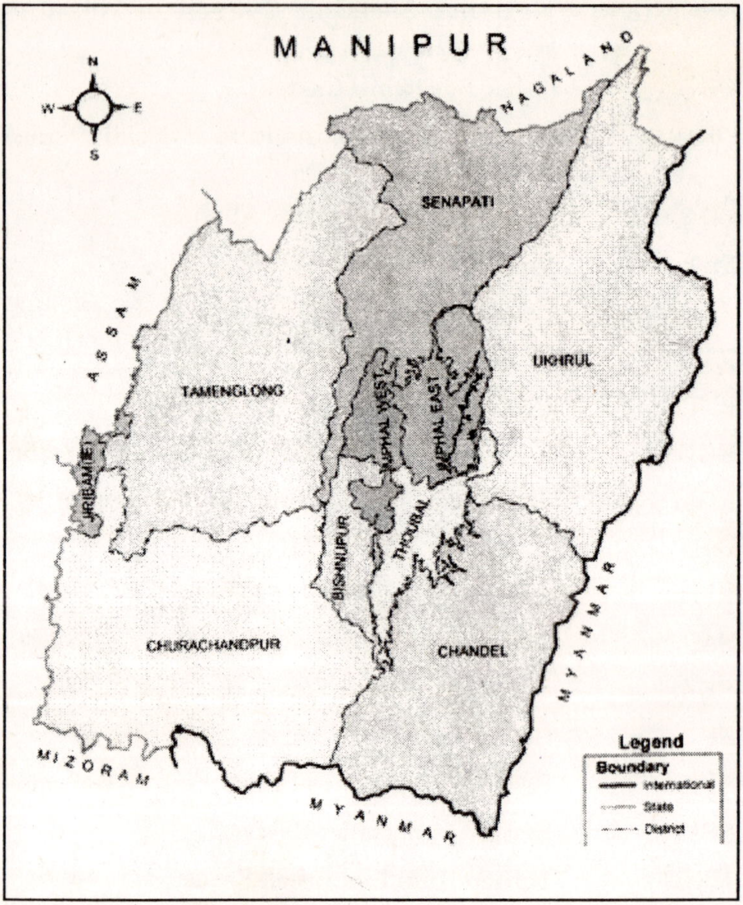
MANIPUR
N
W
E
S
NAGALAND
SENAPATI
ASSAM
TAMENGLONG
UKHRUL
IMPHAL WEST
IMPHAL EAST
JIRIBAM
BISHNUPUR
THOUBAL
CHURACHANDPUR
CHANDEL
MYANMAR
MIZORAM
MYANMAR
Legend
Boundary
International
State
District

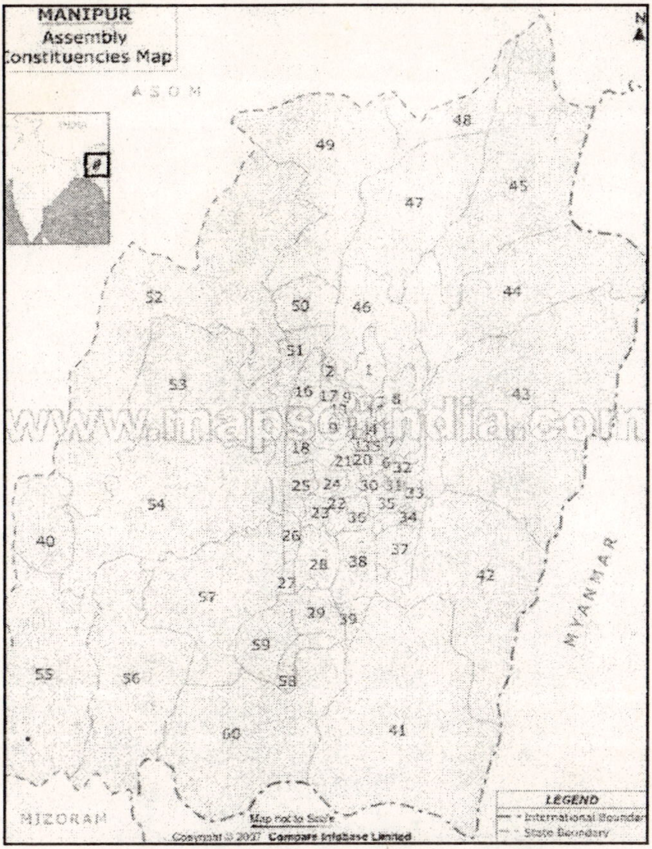

Manipur Assembly Constituencies

1. Khundrakpam
2. Heingang
3. Khurai
4. Khetrigao
5. Thongju
6. Keirao
7. Andro
8. Lamlai
9. Thangmeiband
10. Uripok
11. Sagolband
12. Keishamthong
13. Singjamei
14. Yaishkul
15. Wangkhei
16. Sekmai (SC)
17. Lamsang
18. Konthoujam
19. Patsoi
20. Langthabal
21. Naoriya Pakhanglakpa
22. Wangoi
23. Mayang Imphal
24. Nambol
25. Oinam
26. Bishenpur
27. Moirang
28. Thanga
29. Kumbi
30. Lilong
31. Thoubal
32. Wangkhem
33. Heirok
34. Wabgjing Tentha
35. Khangabok
36. Wabgai
37. Kakching
38. Hiyanglam
39. Sungnoo
40. Jiribam
41. Chandel (ST)
42. Tengnoupal (ST)
43. Phungyar (ST)
44. Ukhrul (ST)
45. Chingai (ST)
46. Saikul (ST)
47. Karong (ST)
48. Mao (ST)
49. Tadubi (ST)
50. Kangokpl
51. Saitu (ST)
52. Tamei (ST)
53. Tamenglong (ST)
54. Nungba (ST)
55. Tipaimukh (ST)
56. Thanlong (ST)
57. Henglep (ST)
58. Churachandpur (ST)
59. Saikot (ST)
60. Singhat (ST)

1

INTRODUCTION

Elections attract not only political practitioners, grassroots workers of all political parties and the electorate but also social scientists for the thrill, sensation, stakes and values associated with the entire process. Elections at all levels, national, regional and local, register a series of processes and stages right from the announcement of the election dates to the poll verdict, each one of which is crucial and nerve-wrecking. There is an involvement of stakes for parties, their leaders and workers as also the future of a given political setting. Therefore, in all democracies, elections stand as the culmination of countless political activities pursued by the concerned individuals and parties for a considerable period of time, notwithstanding the difference in the magnitude of involvement and concern at various levels. Considering the importance of each and every election because of the involvement of various degrees and manifestations of power, various shades and sections of the society, including the print and the electronic media try to play their respective roles.[1] That is why academics, too, find every election interesting, of course, for reasons entirely different from others. The dynamics of elections are varied and intriguing. The results, whether fractured or decisive, are suggestive of future political arrangements and alignments of forces that matter in the affairs of a nation.

Among the distinct and pronounced stages of an election process such as the announcement of date of the election, the nomination process, articulation of issues, nature of campaign, and finally the act of voting, three stages are considered to be most important – the articulation of issues, the campaign, and the act of voting. The answer to the question as to why the voters accord preference to a candidate or a party could be found in the mechanism that moulds the issues and carry them to the electorate through campaign. Two models provide tentative explanation as to how position-issues finally play a decisive role in any election. The directional model suggests that a successful campaigner carries strong message to the voters that eventually leads to convincing victory in the elections.[2] The alternative, called the 'proximity model' insists that political parties tend to support centrist policies to score electoral victory.[3] In the context of India and other South Asian countries the first model appears to be more relevant. Issues and campaign constitute the core of all elections – whether national, state or local.

Surprises strike almost every Indian election – whether for the Lok Sabha or for Assembly. Despite speculations engineered by media and other agencies, election results reflect determined people's response to the current political situation in a given setting and signal the future trends in politics. While some of the elections in India were epoch-making, as in the case of the general elections of 1977, culminating the internal emergency and also the one-party domination in the country. Contrary to the speculations made by political pundits and media establishments, the outcome of the 2004 Lok Sabha elections, which brought a Congress-led coalition to power, baffled everyone. The miscalculation of the psephologyists suggests that they either failed to read voters' mind correctly or were carried away by falsification of current trend, engineered by the apparently focused and favoured parties in media's good book.

Manipur State Assembly elections held in 2007 too stood conspicuous by the unfolding of latent trends having far reaching consequences. Like other previous elections this election too was marred by pre and post election violence. Not everyone was stunned by the overwhelming turn out of the electorate on the days of the three-phased elections, for, high voting turnout has been a regular hallmark in the political process in Manipur. What stunned everyone was that the Congress returned to power, for the second consecutive term with an emphatic majority.

Panoramic View of Manipur

Manipur, also called "Switzerland of the East" is a land-locked state situated in the extreme corner of the North Eastern part of India. It is situated between 93.03^{0}E-94.78^{0}E longitude and 23.83^{0}N-25.68^{0}N latitude. It is somewhat rectangular in shape with two distinct areas, the Hills and the Plains. The geographical area of the state is 22,356 sq.km comprising only 0.68 per cent of the total land surface of the whole country. The oval shaped valley located in the center of Manipur accounts for 1,862 sq.km, which is 10 per cent only, while the hilly region constitutes 90 per cent of the total land area of the state.

The state has a long border of about 854 km, of which 425 km is international touching Upper Myanmar and its Chin Hills, and the rest 502 km touches Nagaland, Assam and Mizoram. The state is bounded in the South by Mizoram, in the North by Nagaland and in the West by the Cachar district of Assam.

The state's river system flows from North to South. There are two main rivers, eight small rivers and numerous streamlets. The two main rivers are the Imphal river and the Barak river which play an important role in the economy of the state. The Imphal river irrigates the valley districts and flows into Myanmar through Chin Hills and finally flows into the Chindwin river of that country. The Barak river serves as the only means of communication for the inaccessible Tamenglong district and the Jiribam sub-division of Imphal East district. It passes through the western hill region of the state and then flows through the Cachar valley.

Manipur has nine revenue districts *viz.* Imphal West, Imphal East, Bishenpur, Thoubal, Senapati, Tamenglong, Ukhrul, Churachandpur and Chandel. Out of these nine districts, four are confined to valley areas and the rest are in the hill areas. When Manipur became a full fledged state on January 21, 1972 after its merger with India in September 1949, the Assembly constituencies were also delimited in the same year to 60 constituencies out of which 19 are reserved for Scheduled Tribes and one for Scheduled Caste. Imphal is the Capital of the state, the hub of all socio-political and economic activities.

The Demographic Profile

Manipur is a polyglot state. The question of the origin of the people of this land is still quite obscure. R.B. Pemberton opined that the Manipuris were the descendants of a Tatar colony, which probably emigrated from the north-west border of China during the sanguinary conflicts for supremacy between the different members of the Chinese and the Tatar dynasties, in the 13th and 14th centuries.[4] It is also believed that the Manipuris descended from an Indo-Chinese stock with some admixture of Aryan blood derived from successive waves of Aryan invaders that had passed along the Gangetic and the Brahmaputra valley in the pre-historic times.[5] In the recent past, a couple of Manipur scholars of the Sanskritization persuasion identified her with the Manipura of *Mahabharata*, claiming the people of this land to be descendants of Babribhma and Chitrangada. But there is hardly any reliable Indological account of this claim.

At present, the population of Manipur is divided into (i) Meiteis (Hindu Vaishnavites) who constitute about 60 per cent of the population inhabiting the valley areas along with Pangals (Manipuri Muslims), constituting about 8 per cent of the population, and (ii) the different 29 tribes living in the hilly regions. The tribes of Manipur may be divided into two broad types - the Nagas and the Kukis. Besides, there are small communities such as Marwaris, Bengalis, Punjabis, Biharis, Sikhs, Tamils and Nepalese; they are late-comers to the state. Anyway, all these communities constitute a pluralistic Manipuri society.

According to the 2001 Census the total population of Manipur is 23,88,634. Out of this 12,07,338 are males and 11,81,296 females. The four valley districts accommodate 14,05,560 population while the hill districts have a population of 9,83,074. Table 1.1 indicates the trend of population growth in the state since 1901.

Table 1.1
Basic demographic statistics of Manipur
(1901-2001)

Year	*Total Population*			*Variation Persons*	*Decadel percentage variation*	*Density of population per sq. km*	*Sex ratio female per 1000 males*
	Male	*Female*	*Total*				
1901	139632	144833	28465	-	-	13	1037
1911	170666	175556	346222	61757	21.71	16	1029
1921	188119	195879	384016	37794	10.98	17	1041
1931	215815	229791	445606	61590	16.04	20	065
1941	249183	262886	512069	66463	14.92	23	1055
1951	283685	293950	577635	65566	12.80	26	1036
1961	387058	392979	780037	202402	35.04	40	1015
1971	541675	531078	1072753	292716	37.53	48	980
1981	721006	699947	142953	348200	32.46	64	971
1991	938359	898790	1837149	416196	29.73	82	958
2001	1207338	1181296	2388634	551485	30.02	107	978

Source: Directorate of Census Operation, Manipur

Table 1.2

Religion-wise percentage of population in North East (1991-2001)

States	*Hindus*		*Muslims*		*Christians*		*Buddhists*	
	1991	*2001*	*1991*	*2001*	*1991*	*2001*	*1991*	*2001*
Assam	67.1	64.9	28.4	30.9	3.3	3.7	-	0.2
Arunachal Pradesh	37.0	34.6	-	1.9	-	18.7	12.9	13.0
Meghalaya	14.7	13.3	-	4.3	64.6	70.3	-	0.2
Manipur	57.7	46.0	7.3	8.8	34.1	34.0	-	0.1
Mizoram	5.0	3.6	-	1.1	85.7	87.0	7.8	7.9
Nagaland	10.1	7.7	1.7	1.8	87.5	90.0	-	0.1
Tripura	86.5	85.6	7.1	8.0	-	3.2	4.7	3.1

Source: *Census of India*

Table 1.1 shows that since the decade of 1951-1961, the growth rate of population in Manipur has been higher than the all-India average. It is interesting to mention here that during the decade, 1991-2001, the growth of Hindu and Christian population has declined from 57.7 to 46 per cent and from 34.1 to 34.0 per cent respectively. On the other hand, the growth of Muslim population in the state has increased from 7.3 in 1991 to 8.8 per cent in 2001. The religion-wise comparison of population in the North-eastern States is shown below as Table 1.2.

Table 1.3 for the religion-wise breakup of the population of Manipur in the 9 districts shows the overall picture of the state in demographic geography of the various religious communities. It clearly indicates that the Hill districts have a higher concentration of Christians, while the Hindus predominantly inhabit the valley. It is also noteworthy that the majority of the people of Manipur live in the plain districts of the valley, despite the fact that the valley constitutes only 9 per cent of the total land-area of the state. It also presents the hill-valley divide on religious count. The ongoing insurgency-related situation may, therefore, have a religious dimension, which however has not been so far examined.

One of the notable aspects in the distribution of population relates to density. The Census 2001 records that it is 107 persons in per sq. km. While the population density in the valley is 628 sq. km, it is 49 in the hill areas. The following table (Table 1.4) shows the district-wise population of Manipur.

Table 1.3

District-wise breakup of religious composition of the population of Manipur in %

Districts	*Total*	*Hindus*	*Muslims*	*Christians*	*Sikh*	*Buddhist*	*Jain*
Senapati	208406	15.11	.03	83.23	.007	.34	.01
Tamenglong	86278	1.81	.17	97.49	.01	.55	-
Churachandpur	176184	5.61	.70	93.34	.10	-	.002
Chandel	71014	10.55	1.99	86.16	.28	.09	.03
Ukhrul	109275	5.99	.26	93.67	.02	.06	.02
Hill Districts	**651157**	**8.76**	**.49**	**98.92**	**.067**	**.08**	**.01**
Imphal East	330460	79.01	14 7	5.3	.03	.02	*
Imphal West	380801	91.75	3.56	2.55	.02	.02	*
Bishnupur	180773	88.04	6.10	5.37	.02	*	*
Thoubal	293958	79.41	19.45	.94	.01	*	*
Valley Districts	**1185992**	**84.52**	**10.99**	**3.46**	**.08**	*	*

Source : Statistical Abstract: Manipur 2005

*Nil or less than .01 per cent

Table 1.4

District-wise distribution of population of Manipur

State/District	*Total population*		*Sex Ratio*		*Density*	*Decadal*
	Persons	*Males*	*Females*	*Females*	*per sq.km*	*growth rate*
I. Valley Districts	1405560	702767	702793	1000	628	-
Imphal West	439532	218941	220585	1007	847	15.42
Imphal East	393480	197710	196070	992	555	19.16
Bishnupur	205907	102772	103135	1004	415	13.90
Thoubal	366341	183338	183003	998	713	24.62
II. Hill Districts	**983074**	**504571**	**478503**	**948**	**49**	-
Senapati	379214	196646	182568	928	116	81.96
Tamenglong	111493	57994	53499	922	25	29.23
Churachandpur	228707	111740	113967	993	50	29.81
Ukhrul	140946	73413	675333	920	31	28.98
Chandel	122714	61778	60936	986	37	72.80
Manipur	2388634	1207338	1181296	978	107	30.02

Source: Census of India 2001.

From the above Table, one finds that Imphal West has the highest density of population among the districts, with 847 persons per sq.km, while Tamenglong district has the lowest, with 25 persons per sq. km. Census 2001 reveals that the population in the valley districts stands at 14,05,560 while the hill district has a population of 9,83,074. It may be mentioned here that there is no census data on the breakup of the tribal population of the state in 1991 and 2001 census.

The state's urban population stands at 570,410 as per 2001 Census against 505,645 in 1991 and the rural population stand at 1,818,224 as against 1,331,504 in 1991. It shows that out of the total population 76.12 per cent lives in the rural areas and only 23.88 per cent, in the urban areas.

Manipur is one of the low performing states of the country, if a few indicators such as percentage of population living below poverty line, per capita income, state GDP and other associated factors, infrastructure such as roads and communication network, power supply are taken into account. Chapter II devotes itself to a brief presentation of the relevant data on the economic scenario. It might help understand the difficult economic situation facing the state. What ails Manipur's economy has a relation with the political scenario of the state. Underdevelopment, stagnation in the economy, lack of industrial development and poor performance in all sectors create conditions for political instability and make the political landscape fertile for the rise of militancy.

The Political Scenario

Manipur had been ruled by monarchs, as *Royal Manipur Chronicle* records, since 33 AD. Nongda Lairen

Pakhangba of Ningthouja dynasty was the first king of Manipur. Since then 76 kings ruled till 1891, when the British finally took over Manipur under its direct control and put king Churachand as a titular monarch, who was then a minor, under the protection of the British Government. The British presence in the state was a sequel to the first Anglo-Burmese war of 1824-1826 which led to the conclusion of the Yandaboo treaty on February 24, 1826 (See Appendix II). The Treaty recognized the independence of the kingdom of the then ruler Gambhir Singh. With his death and succession of his eldest son Chandrakriti Singh in 1886, palace intrigues among the ten brothers destabilized the institution of monarchy and eventually led to the Anglo-Manipur War of 1891.[6] The war virtually ended the independent status of Manipur. The king became a titular authority and the British officers exercised the real power. When the British left India in 1947, Manipur once again regained its sovereignty under its ruler Bodhchandra.[7] Then followed certain nerve-wrecking developments, such as framing the Manipur State Constitution Act, 1947 and signing the Manipur Merger Agreement (See Appendix III) on September 21,1949 at Shillong, which were destined to have far reaching consequences including the current insurgency situation in the state. The merger was followed by dissolution of the state Assembly, which had 53 seats. Manipur became a Part C State, to be administered by the President of India through a Chief Commissioner or a Lieutenant Governor. On November 1, 1956 it ceased to be a Part C State and became a Union Territory with a Territorial Council comprising 30 elected members and 2 nominated Members. It was a prelude to Manipur's statehood in 1972. The Territorial Council was converted into the Territorial Legislative

Assembly with the same composition fixed in June 1963. With the enactment of the North-Eastern Areas (Reorganisation Act, 1971), Manipur was granted the status of full statehood on January 21, 1972 with a 60 member Legislative Assembly.

It is widely believed that had the Government of India conferred on Manipur the status of statehood, latest by 1963 instead of converting the Territorial Council into a Territorial Legislative Assembly, the state would have experienced a healthy parliamentary culture and gained the benefit of political empowerment. This could have resulted in the political development on a positive line. As B.G. Verghese writes succinctly:

> There was a deep sense of hurt that, despite its long and unbroken history as a distinctive if not always independent political entity, Manipur was not only denied the autonomy it sought, with maybe a Kashmir-like Article 370 status, but had to agonise for a full 23 years before it was granted statehood within the Indian Union, a status accorded to Nagaland, Meghalaya and Himachal.[8]

Political instability surfaced as early as March 1967 when M. Koireng Singh took over as the Chief Minister for the second term. Thereafter, the afflictions of floor-crossing, horse-trading, frequent change of Chief Ministers and dissolution of Assembly became the order of the day in the political process in Manipur.[9]

Politics of Defection in Manipur: The hallmark of instability

The chequered political history of Manipur marked by endemic problems of instability started in 1963 when the Territorial Council was upgraded to the status of a Territorial Assembly and M. Koireng Singh was appointed as the Chief Minister. However, the internal feud within the Congress party did not surface until 1967, when the Fourth General Election held. It is a reflection of the national scene soon after the fourth general elections when intra-party conflicts surfaced and the political landscape was radically changed leading eventually to the split of the Congress.[10] Though Congress was able to form the government by being the majority party with 16 members and with the support of 7 Independents, the politics of defection hung as the Damocles Sword on the M. Koireng Singh ministry. In seven months since he became the Chief Minister for the second time, 9 of his party colleagues deserted him, staging a defection. The ministry was reduced to a minority and it had no option but to resign in October 1967. From this political turnabout the process of ministry-making and ministry-breaking continued unabated with occasional punctuation by President's Rule. With no political formation winning a clear majority in the House in subsequent years, the government formation process in Manipur hinged on defections and splits.[11]

In a span of 35 years, 1967-2002, Manipur has seen eight Chief Ministers (Appendix I) but none of them completed a full term. Manipur had earned a dubious record of as many as 25 ministries within this period of time due mainly to the politics of defection and floor crossing. Chief Ministers and governments have changed no less than 16 times. Two Chief Ministers changed their party affiliations three times within a short span of time. Some coalition partners changed their parties three times in 48 hours.[12] Added to this, the picture of political instability is complete with the imposition of six spells of President's Rule. On two occasions, President's Rule was imposed after dissolving the Assembly. The Assembly was kept in suspended animation on four other occasions.[13] "Perhaps," it is argued, "no other state in the country has ever witnessed such an unstable political climate as that of Manipur. Changes of party loyalty, shifting alliances, both in the individual and collective levels are so frequent and ruthless that the state has witnessed ever since it became a full-fledged state in 1972 as many as eight Chief Ministers with frequent change of guards on 18 occasions."[14]

Defection, horse-trading and shifting of loyalties, which became an integral part of party politics in Manipur, have been the bane to the state's politics. Several legislators have been suspended for violating the anti-defection law, but that has not deterred others from switching allegiance during a political crisis. In 1997, a group of Ministers and MLAs led by former Speaker, Nipamacha Singh broke away from the ruling Congress headed by Rishang Keishing and floated the Manipur State Congress Party (MSCP), which subsequently formed the government. It was a direct challenge to the anti-defection legislation. Defection was rampant till 2002, when some semblance of stability was instilled resulting in the completion of the full term of the ministry headed by Okram Ibobi Singh.

Pattern in the Fall of Governments through Defections in Manipur from 1967

1) In October 1967, 9 Congress members defected from M. Koireng Singh ministry reducing the strength from 23 to 14. As a result, ministry had to resign. L. Thambou Singh became the Chief Minister for 12 days only. M. Koireng engineered another defection to topple his denigrators from

the seat of power in less than two weeks. President's rule was imposed, as no party was able to form a stable government.

2) Within three months after the imposition of President's Rule, M. Koireng Singh could regroup the Congress MLAs and stage a come back to form the government on February 19, 1968. But on September 10, 1969, 12 Congressmen resigned from the party and formed a United Legislature Party (ULP) under the leadership of Md. Alimuddin, with the support of 4 Sanghata Socialist Party (SSP) members and one from the Communist Party of India (CPI) and 3 Independents. But the constant defections from the Congress and the Independents made it impossible to have a viable coalition government. As a result, the Central Government again imposed President's Rule in the state from October 1969 till the Fifth General Elections in March 1972.[15]

3) In the Fifth Assembly elections, the Manipur People's Party (MPP) with 15 members along with 3 Socialists, 3 Congress (O) members, 10 Independents and a Congress defector formed the government under the leadership of Md. Alimuddin on March 20, 1972. Later on, in November 1972 the ULP increased its strength to 36 members, by masterminding defections. However, on March 15, 1973, as many as 9 UPL members crossed the floor and joined the Opposition to constitute the Progressive Democratic Alliance (PDA) under the leadership of Atikho Daiho of the Congress. The Alimuddin government with 26 members was reduced to minority.

In his report to the Governor, the Chief Minister observed that "two defectors had the record of changing sides four times each and both of them were Congressmen, while some Congress members defected thrice". He concluded: "In the counter-defections the support by some defectors to any ministry is bound to be extremely fake and unreal". Subsequently, Alimuddin had to resign along with his ministry on March 26, 1973, following an acrimonious debate on a no-confidence motion in the Assembly. The Governor, while forwarding the note of the Chief Minister, observed in his report: "It is true that in a legislature in which 18 members have changed sides within a period of one year there is no certainty that any government will be stable". The end result was that President's Rule was imposed for the third time in Manipur and the Legislative Assembly was dissolved on March 28, 1973.[16]

4) In the Assembly Elections of January 1980 no party could get a majority and a coalition government of the Congress (I), the Congress (U), the MPP and Independents under the leadership of R.K. Dorendra Singh was sworn in on January 17, 1980. But, sometime later, the Manipur National Democratic Party (MNDP) was formed by some members who had defected from their respective parties, merged with the MPP bringing instability to the ministry of Dorendra Singh. He too could not complete the full term of his ministry.

5) In a game of defection, floor-crossing and horse trading, Rishang Keishing became the Chief Minister for a record of fifth time, notwithstanding the fact that he could never ever complete a full term. Dorendra Singh too had been the Chief Minister for four times and like Keishing he, too, could not complete a full term.

Besides, the defections mentioned above that perpetuated instability in the government formation in Manipur, splits, internal bickering, switching alliance and passing no-confidence motion became regular and routine affairs in state politics in Manipur especially after the Assembly elections of 1990. The situation did not change till 2002. After the elections held in 2000 no party was able to get a simple majority. A coalition government led by W. Nipamacha Singh was formed in which the BJP and the Samata Party were the main players. Internal bickering, defections and political gimmicks crippled the coalition. Finally, the BJP, a partner in the Nipamacha ministry, pulled out of the government and allowed it to fall like a house of cards. The ministry formed with divergent groups could not complete its term. As a result, the mid-term poll was held in February 2002. The murky politics of Manipur as aptly described by a retired politician: "Power - the first love of every politician is a treacherous belove. Like those of pretty women of little virtues, her wooers are many and her loyalties shifting" remained the same for four decades.

Manipur is one of the most trouble-torn states in North East India. It is believed that political instability in the state has a direct relationship with insurgency situation. A fractured Assembly and a Government always haunted by the spectre of surgical dismissal, could hardly handle the situation, plagued by perennial problems arising out of secessionist and other inter-ethnic armed movements. Political situation in Manipur, over the years, has drifted from bad to worse. However, the Assembly elections in 2007 had thrown a ray of hope for the state. The present Government does not suffer from an instability syndrome, indicating thereby that stability might give peace a chance and that insurgency could prove to be a matter of the past, provided, of course, that the Government proves to be a performing and responsible one. That is why the Assembly elections of 2007 became so important, besides other issues, which figured during the electioneering; the huge turnout of the electorate added significance.

Insurgency Situation

North East India has been experiencing a steady increase in the number of militant groups and their activities since the early 1950s when Angami Zapu Phizo fired the first salvo for armed secession in the present state of Nagaland. Gradually Assam, Manipur, Mizoram and Tripura became the victims of insurgency of grave import. Manipur's insurgency and armed movements have a long history. The political profile of Manipur cannot be outlined and understood without discussing the insurgency situation in the state. The following section devotes itself to a brief presentation.

Soon after the Independence, the Imphal valley was rocked by a communist movement led by Hijam Irabat Singh.[17] It was a short-lived armed struggle (1948-51), which failed to make a mark in the political history of Manipur. There was a spillover impact of the secessionist movement initiated spearheaded by Phizo in Nagaland

and continued by the National Socialist Council of Nagaland (NSCN), Isac-Muivah faction in the Naga dominated areas of Manipur; it was followed by the Kukis in some of the hill districts and by the Meiteis in the Imphal Valley. It is argued that the deep sense of dissatisfaction in the mind of the Meiteis owing to the circumstances leading to the signing of the merger document by the Maharaja of Manipur under alleged duress, on September 21, 1949, was one of the principal reasons behind the insurgency upsurge in the Imphal Valley.[18]

Manipur has seen some major secessionist movements, launched by various ethnic communities residing in the state. The major ones are the Meitei, the Naga and the Kuki insurgencies. The Naga insurgent groups – the National Socialist Council of Nagaland (Isak-Muivah) (NSCN-IM) and the National Socialist Council of Nagaland (Khaplang) (NSCN-K) are also active in the Naga inhabited areas in four of Manipur's five hill districts, namely, Ukhrul, Senapati, Tamenglong and Chandel. The NSCN-IM used Ukhrul district particularly, where its leader T. Muivah was born, as a base for collecting funds and its recruiting cadres. It carried out several terrorist activities in the state in the 1990s. Similarly, a number of Kuki outfits are also active in the Churachandpur district. The Kuki National Army (KNA) has been fighting for a sovereign 'Kukiland', comprising some parts of India and Myanmar through an armed struggle, while the Kuki National Front (KNF) and a number of other similar groups have launched armed struggle for a separate state within the Indian Union. The armed conflict between the Nagas and the Kukis beginning in 1992 had an added dimension, since it was also a bitter struggle to control land and drug trafficking through the border town of Moreh, in the Chandel district of Manipur.[19] Besides, three other ethnic groups and some others too, such as the Paite, the Hmar, the Vaiphei, and the Muslims, have launched their own insurgent outfits in recent years. As a result, the Imphal Valley has become a hub of militant activities for many insurgent groups.[20]

Imphal valley, comprising four districts - Imphal East, Imphal West, Bishnupur and Thoubal, is the very pulse of Manipur, and the meeting point of diverse socio-cultural and ethnic identities. It spreads over an area of about 2,238 sq.kms, roughly about ten per cent of the State's land area which is 22,356 sq.km. [21] The valley has been experiencing tumultuous violence for the last five decades. The majority of the 20 odd insurgent outfits of Manipur are active in the valley. Besides the aforementioned insurgent groups, some others which are considerably active in the valley are, the United National Liberation Front (UNLF), the Revolutionary People's Front (RPF) and its armed wing the People's Liberation Army (PLA), the People's Revolutionary Party of Kangleipak (PREPAK), the Kanglei Yawol Kanna Lup (KYKL), the Kangleipak Communist Party (KCP), and the People's United Liberation Front (PULF), which is an essentially Muslim militant organization. It is estimated that about 9,070 insurgents operate in the valley area. [22]

The Upsurge: Causes

The rise of secessionist movements and other forms of insurgency especially in the lush-green and fertile valley is due to some historical factors, besides a perceived sense of deprivation and neglect by the Indian state in the post independence era. From a small beginning in the early 1940s, the Communists under Hijam Irabot Singh launched a full-blown revolutionary movement in 1948 to liberate Manipur from the feudalism and semi-colonialism of the Manipur Kings and as also from the Indian state. Their objectives were to install a popular responsible people's government, to implement land reform in order to ensure land entitlement to the landless peasants and to revise land revenue policy, and ensure the right to self-determination. Though Irabot Singh's cause to fight for an independent socialist republic of Manipur, could not advance further due to his death in 1951, the revolutionary seeds sown by him had not fallen on barren ground.[23] He left behind a legacy for future revolutionaries, for mobilizing indigenous people to secure a space in the insurgency-afflicted history of Manipur. The dissident armed elements amongst Irabot's comrades retained their weapons of World War II vintage. That provided an emotional, military and psychological strength to pursue their armed struggle against their targets associated with Indian Union.[24] Therefore, the rise of political consciousness with a secessionist ideology, the controversial merger agreement, in addition to the latent feeling of relative deprivation laid the foundation for the emergence of a number of insurgent groups, and provided the ostensible 'logic' to justify their armed struggle against the Indian state.

As already stated, the merger of Manipur in a controversial manner with the Indian Union left a deep sense of hurt, as Manipur has a long and unbroken history as a distinctive political entity. It appears that insurgency in the valley started with a curious chemistry of leftist ideals and a nationalistic fervor against the attitude of the Indian Government, which, in common perception, was seen to have forcibly taken over Manipur, through signing the merger document under alleged duress. Compounded with the feeling of dissatisfaction among the Meiteis, who constitute around 50 per cent of the total population, at the forced merger, a deep-rooted sense of alienation could be found among them, when compared with the caste Hindus in other parts of India. The belief in the rest of India that all Mongoloid looking people or with Mongoloid descent are tribal people, as allegedly evident in the Indian metropolis in the attitude and behaviour shown to these Northeasterners, often hurt the sentiments of the Meiteis. It goes without underscoring that the Meiteis are plain settlers and mostly Gauriya Vaishnavite Hindus. Yet, the difference in treatment with other caste Hindus of India, compared to the Meitei Vaishnavite Hindus appears to be humiliation to the latter. The putative impression that the Meiteis are looked down upon by the rest of the Hindus in India ignited the secessionist sentiments that started growing in the 1960s and 1970s among the youth of the Manipuri society. This forced them to take guns against the Indian Union and work for a sovereign independent Manipur. In the 1960s, when the Naga insurgency in the Hills of Manipur was at its peak, the Meiteis realized that they had become a target of Naga attack, as they, along with the Hindus of the rest of India, were being identified as symbol of the Central government and of exploitation. This was somewhat an uncomfortable conjecture which compounded the worries and distress of the Meitei youths, who felt that the sharing of the common identity symbol, that of being Hindu, with the rest of the country, did not bring any visible economic gains to them. The Union Government, in its bid to win over the underground elements, is alleged to have shown preferential treatment to the people in the hill areas of the state, at the cost of the Imphal valley. This approach generated a sense of relative deprivation among the Meitei youth. A strong political consciousness, with a tinge of cultural nationalism started developing in the minds of the educated Meitei youth, who got themselves emotionally involved in the movement for Meitei identity. Such a feeling led to the formation of the now proscribed the UNLF in 1964. Also, the armed strike by the PLA in 1978, under N. Bisheswar, as a subsequent development of this trend of political action created a huge problem of insurgency in Manipur.

Adding woes to the wounds, the economic scenario of the state has been pathetic all along as outlined in Chapter II, with large-scale unemployment, rural poverty and almost total absence of industrialization in the state. The Fifth Five Year Plan, 1974-79 of Manipur, makes the candid confession that "unlike many other advanced states of the Indian Union, Manipur has achieved the statehood 25 years behind others and, therefore, she has to take the course of speedy development which many other states made in 1947".[25] Under the circumstances, a mindset has developed among the youths that Manipur is a small state, neglected and easily oppressed by a dominating Indian nation.

By the late 1970s and early 80s insurgency was at its height. It was in those days that Chinese red paper balloons called 'chebons' were being distributed in Manipur to communicate the message of a deep-rooted sense of deprivation and dissatisfaction among the common masses, along with a call for defiance against the Union Government. Around the same time the PLA started its urban insurgency counted amongst highly organized and effective ones in South Asia. In 1980-81, large areas of Imphal Valley were under their indirect control. They acclaimed to be the perfect examples of Maoist guerrilla fighters, in fact, ushered in India's first spell of urban insurgency and Asia's second, after Saigon.[26]

Consequences

The response of the Indian state to the perceived notion of negligence, however, has not been very encouraging. India's delayed response to insurgency related incidents, least concern for the economic development of the state, inconclusive decision-making and evasion of responsibility in negotiations multiplied problems. All this reinforced people's mistrust of the policy makers at the Centre. In fact, the insurgency movements have posed an enormity of challenge to the sovereignty and territorial integrity of the Indian nation. The intensity and duration of these movements indicate the Manipuri insurgent's ability and endurance. The seriousness in the commitment of the Union Government towards conflict management and conflict transformation as also the methodology adopted are put under the scanner.

The protracted conflict has resulted in the horizontal proliferation of insurgent groups and vertical increase in their armed and violent activities. It has resulted in fragmentation and fractionalization within and amongst the insurgents. In fact, a vicious cycle of insurgency, military response, lack of investment, collapse of basic services and opportunities serves for regeneration of insurgency. In fact, it has become worse than a vicious cycle, more of a vicious spiral encompassing a syndrome of unmitigated tragedy, and becoming more intractable and complex with each unfortunate turn. As Binalakshmi Nepram writes: "The growing unemployment and corruption, and the deteriorating socio, economic and political situation and the abject lack of development further led to the rise and small arming of other militant outfits".[27]

In the valley areas of Manipur since the days of Hijam Irabot Singh and his Red Guards in 1950 till date, as many as 20 insurgent groups have been operating in Manipur.[28] The chronology of the proliferation of insurgent groups after the formation of UNLF in 1964 goes like this:

- Oinam Sudhir formed the Consolidation Committee of Manipur (CONSCOM) and established the Revolutionary Government of Manipur (RGM) in 1970
- R.K.Tulachandra established the PREPAK in 1977
- The PLA was launched by N.Bisheshwar in 1978
- S. Maipak formed the KCP in 1980
- The KYKL came into being in 1994 by a combination of breakaway groups of the UNLF, the PREPAK and the KCP
- The PULF, the North East Minority Front (NEMF), the Islamic National Front (INF) and the Islamic Liberation Front-Kanglei (ILF-K), known as Manipuri Muslim based outfits, emerged after the Meitei-Pangal clash in 1993.

Chronology of the formation of Hill based insurgent groups:

- The NSCN was established in 1980, which later broke into two factions, one led by Isak Chishi Swu and T.Muivah (NSCN-IM) and the other by S.S.Khaplang (NSCN-K).
- The Kuki National Front (KNF) was formed in 1988 which later broke into two factions KNF-President and KNF-Military Council.
- The Zomi Revolutionary Army (ZRA) with its political wing Zomi Reunification Organisation (ZRO) came into existence in 1993.
- The Kuki National Army with its political wing Kuki National Organization (KNO) appeared in 1998.
- The Hmar People's convention-Democratic (HPC-D), the Kuki Liberation Army (KLA) and the United Kuki Liberation Front (UKLF) are other groups presently operating in the hill areas of the state.

The impact of insurgency in the state has, however, been felt intensely by the people, almost in every aspect of life. The existence of so many militant groups operating in the Imphal valley and the hill areas, has increasingly imperiled the society as a whole. The situation had drifted from bad to worse, during a long period of four decades, owning to installation of governments that were destined to be ineffective and short lived. The situation used to deteriorate when there was no representative government. Manipur has a record of experiencing Presidential rule following political instability, quite often till 2002. In such a situation, the insurgent groups enjoy the privilege of running a parallel administration in the state. More disturbingly, people have also started accepting their *de fecto* authority either out of fear or out of a growing distrust in the administration, or for both. Along with this, the development process has invariably been hampered, as the insurgent groups often siphon off a large chunk of the development fund for procuring arms. And here lies the importance of assessing the economy of insurgency in Manipur, as economy perhaps plays a more important role compared to politics. It is believed that the progressive 'withdrawal' of civil governance and the emergence of a network of collusive arrangements with insurgent outfits, had propelled the growth of a widespread pattern of illegal economic activities that came to be the mainstay and motive for all the insurgencies. A thriving economy of extortion, smuggling, gun-running and an oligo-politic control over government contracts ruled the roost. Indeed, the various 'ideological' factions and rivalries within insurgent movements in the states of North East in general, and Manipur in particular, are often thinly disguised 'turf wars' to retain or gain control over lucrative 'areas of influence', especially the important routes of (illegal) cross border trade, including arms and drug trafficking.

The economic slowdown in Manipur has reduced opportunities for employment, as also the funds for public services, such as health, sanitation, pure drinking water supply and education. Most of its hill districts which are strongholds of insurgents, are reeling under acute poverty, mainly because of under-utilization of natural resources and for want of adequate infrastructure. In Chandel district, over 64 per cent of the people live below poverty line, while in Churachandpur, Ukhrul and Tamenglong districts, it is between 51 and 55 per cent.[29]

Many young men, already frustrated and without employment, are under pressure from insurgent groups to join them, and hence, under suspicion from the security forces. As such, they are highly vulnerable to the risk of arrest and abuse, and consequently, suffer from extreme tension and anxiety. Other family members, including young women, face similar pressures, at risk of harassment and abuse from either side. They suffer from the traumas of losing loved ones in incidents of arrest, encounter, violence and disappearance. With limited employment prospects, educated youths stare at an uncertain future, compounded by fear of violence and excesses resorted to by both the sides; besides, they could be easily lured to join any of the 20+ insurgent outfits. In this process, being frustrated some of them become the victims of drug abuse and HIV/AIDS.

The state is still under a spell of worsened law and order situation with unprecedented insecurity prevailing everywhere. Incidents of failure by state machinery to handle extortion on the Imphal-Moreh national highway, continued terror tactics used by masked gunmen on innocent public, unexplained killings of innocent civilians by security forces, continued kneecapping of erring teachers and principals of school and colleges by insurgent groups like the KYKL, storming of police stations by angry mobs for failure to protect the people, agitations by different associations and organizations etc. have become a part of the social system. The state witnessed over 100 bandhs in 2000 and it cost the state domestic product about Rs. 4, 479 lakhs daily. According to the KYKL, which once banned bandhs and strikes in Manipur in 2003, a single day's bandh in the state leads to a loss of over Rs. 9 crore; and with 72 bandhs in 2001-2002 the cost to the state exchequer was of a mind-boggling Rs. 676.48 crores.[30]

Meanwhile, insurgent outfits like the KYKL, the RPF have also started various populist measures for gaining the support of the people and legitimisation of its organisation. For instance, such groups have started certain anti-corruption measures, including penalizing the people involved in corrupt practices and drugs trafficking.

Questions of human security

Kofi Annan stated "Human security, in its broadest sense, embraces far more than the absence of violent conflict. It encompasses human rights, good governance, access to education and health care and ensuring that each individual has opportunities and choices to fulfill his or her potential. Every step in this direction is also a steep towards reducing poverty, achieving economic growth and preventing conflict. Freedom from want, freedom from fear, and the freedom of future generations to inherit a healthy natural environment — these are the interrelated building blocks of human – and therefore national – security."[31] Human security can no longer be understood in purely military terms. Rather, it must encompass economic development, social justice, environmental protection, democratization, disarmament, and respect for human rights and the rule of law. Looking at the overall insurgency scenario in Manipur, which has been reeling under protracted armed conflict of almost five decades, deteriorating law and order situation, killing spree by various insurgent groups against their fellow insurgents and innocent civilians, gross human rights violations committed by the insurgents as well as the security forces, arbitrary arrests under certain draconian laws like Armed Forces Special Power's Act, (AFSPA) 1958 and National Security Act (NSA), instances of custodial deaths, one could be tempted to crisply describe the state as a "killing field". Violence begets violence seems to be the working solution in the present mayhem. Whoever yields the gun power, in the dictum of Mao Zedong, rules the roost in Manipur.

In today's anomic conditions obtaining in Manipur, with increased fractionalization within the society, endless fratricidal factional clashes among insurgent groups have taken a heavy toll of many youths. In order to tackle this unending violence committed by the armed insurgent groups, the state responded to it by declaring Manipur as a Disturbed State in 1980 and use of the provisions of the AFSPA , 1958 (See Appendix III). The Imphal valley was the immediate victim of the proclamation as Disturbed Area and with enforcement of AFSPA, under which many young boys were picked up on mere suspicion - many of them never returned home. This 'historic' step propelled a saga of violence and counter-violence in the state. Enforced disappearance, arbitrary executions, torture, rape, house breaking, looting, arbitrary detention etc. have become a part of day-to-day life. Soon after the enforcement of the AFSPA, about 264 man and women were done to death, 208 were injured. 131 known incidents of Extra Judicial Killings took place in the state.[32] From 1974 to 2004, there were 14 incidents of disappearance of civilians, after by being arrested or picked up by the security forces.[33] Caught between army excesses and violent activities of the ever-proliferating militant outfits, human rights have become an alien category. To many in the state, to be alive itself is great;

for anybody could fall in seconds by a bullet. While army rules in the day time, it is the insurgents who rule at night. In the last 10 years over 5000 people were killed in violence of various types. More than 10 cases of disappearance have been recorded during 1997-1998 alone.[34]

In an atmosphere of recurring political instability, insurgency and anti-insurgency operations, when general elections, either for the Assembly or the Lok Sabha are held, these issues along with others, such as, economic backwardness and unemployment become the most touted ones on the political plank of each and every political party, making the election scenario pretty surcharged with claims and counter-claims. The insurgents' customary call to boycott the national parties seems to be too strong a message to be ignored. Yet, the history of Manipur elections shows emphatically that it is the democratic spirit of the common citizens that overwhelms such threats.

REFERENCES

1. For an impressive understanding of importance of elections in a democratic country see Angus Campbell, *et al., Elections and Political Order* (New York: John Wiley and Sons, 1968).
2. See G. Rabinowitz and S.E. Macdonald, "A directional theory of issue voting", *American Political Science Review*, Vol. 83, No. 1, 1989, pp. 93-121.
3. Oliver Davies *et al.*, "An expository development of a mathematical model of the electoral process", *ibid*, Vol. 64, No. 2, 1970, pp 426-428.
4. For details see R. Boileau Pemberton, *The Eastern Frontier of India*, reprint (New Delhi: Mittal Publications, 2000) and "Muneepoor" in N. Sanajaoba (ed), *Manipur: A British Anthology*, Vol. I (New Delhi: Akansha Publishing House, 2003), pp. 32-63.

5. N.Joykumar Singh, *Social Movements in Manipur*, (New Delhi, Mittal Publications, 1992) p. 19.

6. A number of publications have dealt with the circumstances leading to the Anglo-Manipur War of 1891. For some details see Lal Dena (ed), *History of Modern Manipur: 1826-1949* (New Delhi: Orbit Publishers, 1991) Chapter 3, S.M.A.W. Chishti, *Political Development of Manipur: 1919-1949* (Delhi: Kalpaz Publications, 2005) Chapter 1.

7. See section 7(1)(b) of Indian Independence Act, 1947.

8. B.G. Verghese, *India's Northeast Resurgent: Ethnicity, Insurgency, Governance, Development* (New Delhi: Konark Publishers, 1996) pp. 116.

9. See Appendix I for the tenure of the Chief Ministers of Manipur.

10. For details see Norman D. Palmer, "Fourth General Election", *Asian Survey*, Vol. 7, No. 5, May 1967, pp. 275-291. The argument that elections may have both stabilizing and destabilizing consequences" for any type of political system appears to be valid if one takes the example of Manipur to establish a point that the Assembly elections of 1967 could be treated as the starting point of political instability in the state. For an interesting analysis on the state Assembly elections and their consequences see Norman D. Palmer "Elections and the Political System in India: The 1972 State Assembly Elections and After", *Pacific Affairs*, Vol. 45, No. 4, Winter 1972-73, pp. 535-555, quotation, p. 535.

11. Manipur does not stand on exception. Political defection became the order of the day in many of the states in India soon after the 1967 Lok Sabha elections. See Subhash C. Kashyap, *The Politics of Defection: A Study of State Politics in India* (New Delhi: Continental Publishing House, 1969).

12. For some interesting details see Ved Marwah, "India's Internal Security Challenges", *Strategic Analysis*, Vol. 27, No. 4, October-December 2003, pp 503-515.

13. Kalyan Choudhury, "Fuzzy verdict in Manipur", *The Hindu*, March 4, and 17, 2000.

14. Oinam Bhagat and A. Bimol Akoijam, "Manipur: Assembly Election: Trends and Issues", *Economic and Political Weekly*, February 9, 2002, pp. 519-524.

15. B. Pakem, *Coalition Politics in North-East India* (New Delhi: Regency Publications,1999), p. 88.

16. *ibid*, pp.89-90.

17. Gangmumei Kabui, "Leftist Movement in Manipur: A Case Study of Comrade Irabat Singh", a paper presented in the 35th session of Indian History Congress, Jadavpur University, 1974.

18. Gangmumei Kabui, "Insurgency in Manipur Valley" in B.L. Abbi (ed), *North East Region: Problems and Prospects of Development* (Chandigarh: Centre for Research in Rural and Industrial Development, 1984), pp. 233-234.

19. This is derived from the interviews with a number of scholars and media persons who have deep insight in the insurgency situation in Manipur. However, there is no reliable empirical data on the Naga-Kuki armed conflict.

20. For some details see Aykpam Ibemchal Chanu, *Insurgency Movement in Manipur*, Working Paper Series No. 09 (Guwahati: OKDISCD, 2005).

21. *Statistical Handbook of Manipur*, 2002.

22. Phanjoubam Tarapot, *Bleeding Manipur* (New Delhi: Har-Anand, 2003).

23. Phanjoubam Tarapot, *Insurgency Movement in North-East India* (New Delhi: Vikas Publishing House, 1993).

24. Lokendra Arambam, *Peace Process in Manipur: Armed Conflict, State Repression and Women* (Guwahati: Peace Studies, OKDISCD, 2005).

25. V.I.K. Sarin, *India's North-East in Flames* (New Delhi: Vikas Publishing House, 1982) p.166.

26. Yambem Laba, *"Burma rebels in Manipur"*, *North East Sun*, November 12, 1988, also see Binalakshmi Nepram, *South*

Asia's Fractured Frontier (New Delhi: Mittal Publications, 2002) Chapter 3, pp. 73-81.

27. Binalakshmi Nepram, *ibid,* p. xvi.

28. Phanjoubam Tarapot, *Bleeding Manipur*, n. 22, p.117.

29. Vedaja Sanjenbam, *Manipur: Geography and Regional Development* (New Delhi: Rajesh Publications, 1998) p.118.

30. Oken Jeet Sandham, *Who Rules Manipur's Streets?* Manipuronline.com, Sept. 30, 2005.

31. Kofi Annan. "Secretary-General Salutes International Workshop on Human Security in Mongolia." Two-Day Session in Ulaanbaatar, May 8-10, 2000. Press Release SG/SM/7382, <http://www.un.org/News/Press/docs/2000/20000508.sgsm7382.doc.html> 08/27/01.

32. Chirom Ranjit, *Unrest in Manipur* (Imphal: Chirom Ranjit, 2004) pp.100-121.

33. *ibid*, pp.96-99).

34. *North East Sun*, May 1-4, 1998, Vol.3, No.19, p. 28.

2

ECONOMY OF MANIPUR

A historical glimpse

The economy of the erstwhile princely state of Manipur, mostly agrarian and largely guided by forced labour institutionalized as *Lallup*[1] in history, was to move towards a tax system in 1892, in keeping with the demand for accommodating wide economic needs and business interest. In the event of a tax system being introduced, it was but only evident that the economy got monetized. In this new found monetized economy, though the primary products occupied 80 per cent of the traded goods, industrial products like cloth, yarn and silk came to occupy a sizeable portion of it. In fact, the *Imperial Gazetteer of Manipur* (1909)[2] records that Manipur was China's contemporary in the production of silk. This citation is a pointer to the then prevailing economic structure of Manipur prior to its annexation with the Indian Union in 1949.

Post-1949 too, though agriculture continued to be the mainstay of 99.5 per cent of the rural population in the state, the net area sown per head was only 0.42 acres compared to the all India average of 1.18 acres. It was the number of small-scale establishments that was encouraging. The number of textile establishments was 33, 927 while that of the non-textile establishments was 608 in 1951. It was an economy in which a large segment of the population was guided by an industrial impulse; but this very impulse became the push factor for influx of population from other parts of India in search of greener pastures (Table 2.1). The decade 1951-61 indeed saw a phenomenal increase in the population of the state.[3] The pre-1951 period in Manipur saw the growth of the indigenous skill for economic expansion. The state was able to reap a surplus. However, the influx of population from other parts of India became, arguably, an element of concern for this surplus economy in the post-1951 period. This influx only went on to produce a potential market in Manipur mostly from demand generated in other parts of the country. Though the outflow of resources was a logical consequence followed by the manifestation of indicators of an incarcerated economy, it inevitably led to a widening gulf between the 'haves' and 'have-nots' in the state. By and large, therefore, the overall economic performance was distressing. Although the annual growth rate of the state domestic product was 4.03 per cent, the per capita income recorded a nominal increase of 0.79 per cent only during the period 1960-61 to 1965-66 at 1960-61 prices.

Manipur, as part of the Indian economy, had its own share in the national exercise. The first Five-Year plan had an outlay of Rs.1.55 crore, followed by Rs.6.25 crore in the Second Plan. The total resource committed from the First Plan to the Fourth in the late 60s was Rs.50.93 crore. Viewed against the substantial rise in the value of money from 1960, as a result of inflation in the country, the increase of plan allocation appears nominal. Till 1966, investment was also negligible in the state. In the agriculture sector, the mainstay of the economy, the annual average outlay from 1951-1974 was only Rs.30.62 lakh. In a nutshell, these decades saw failure, not only in the agricultural front but also in the industrial scenario, the latter failing to take off beyond the handloom and silk sectors, which incidentally registered a modest increase. Moreover, till the early 70s, the state seemed to have the least expertise in planning, with plan commitment and budget allocation being unusually low. That no perceptible change took place during the said period was quite apparent.

Table 2.1
Decadal population growth rate in Manipur (in percentage)

Year	*Manipur*	*All India*
1901-11	21.71	5.75
1911-21	10.92	-0.31
1921-31	16.04	11.00
1931-41	14.92	14.22
1941-51	12.80	13.31
1951-61	35.03	21.51
1961-71	37.53	24.80
1971-81	32.46	24.69
1981-91	29.29	23.82
1991-01	24.86	21.34

Source: Census of India

Fig 1: Decadal Growth Rate of Population in Manipur

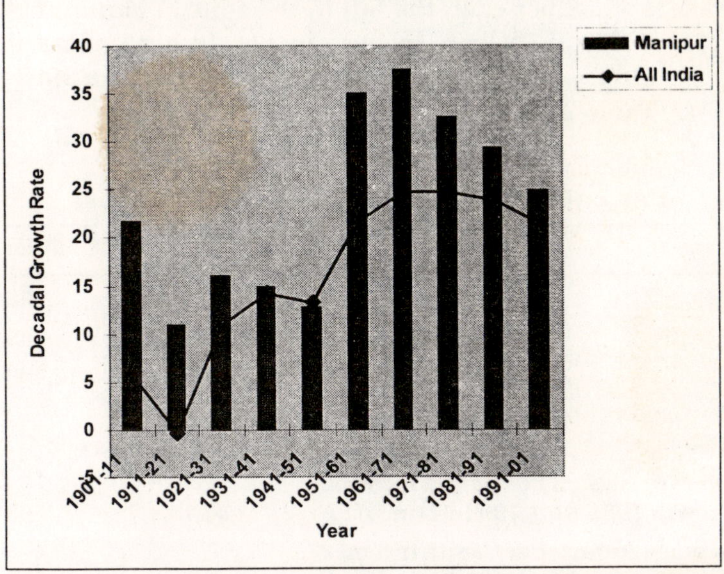

Status of economic development in Manipur: post-1990

The pace of development of Manipur since the beginning of the 90s in the last century, in terms of per capita income, has by and large been almost of the same order as that of the national level. Though Manipur's proportionate growth of per capita income over the period 1994-2002 of 54.24 per cent exceeded the proportionate growth of the national per capita income of around 42.66 per cent over the said period, in fact, in terms of absolute change it lagged behind the per capita income expansion at the national level (Table 2.2). This has been evident in the verity that though the fall in the proportion of rural person falling below the poverty line, as per the official Planning Commission data in 1993-94 of 42.5 per cent was impressive, in relation to the national estimate of decline in rural poverty during 1999-2000 to 27.09 per cent, the fall in the state of Manipur is observably much less. In fact, in absolute numbers it increased from 5.29 lakh in 1987-88 to 7.19 lakh in 1999-2000 (Table 2.3).

Table 2.2
Per capita income in Rs. (1993-94 Prices)

Year	*Manipur*	*All India*
1980-81	4,901	5,966
1993-94	5,811	8,759
2001-02	8,963	12,496
Per Capita Income Change (in Rs) 1994-2002	3,152	3,737
Average Annual Per Capita Income Growth 1980-81 to 1993-94 (in %)	2.43	3.05
Average Annual Per Capita Income Growth 1993-94 to 2001-02 (in %)	3.44	4.19

Source: Statistical Handbook of Manipur, 1980-2002, Directorate of Economics & Statistics Government of Manipur, Imphal

Table 2.3
Poverty level in Manipur

Year	*Manipur*			*All India*		
	Rural	*Urban*	*Total*	*Rural*	*Urban*	*Total*
1973-74	52.67	36.92	49.96	56.44	49.01	54.88
1977-78	59.82	32.71	-	-	-	-
1983-84	42.6	21.73	37.02	-	-	-
1987-88	9.45	31.35	31.35	-	-	-
1993-94	45.94	7.89	33.78	37.27	32.36	35.97
1999-00	42.59	7.95	28.54	27.09	23.62	26.1

* These rural and urban poverty estimates of Manipur are adjusted figures derived by assuming the proportion between Manipur and Assam poverty

Source: Economic Survey, Government of Manipur, Statistical Abstract of Manipur, Planning Commission Quoted by the Indian Economic Survey, 2001-2002.

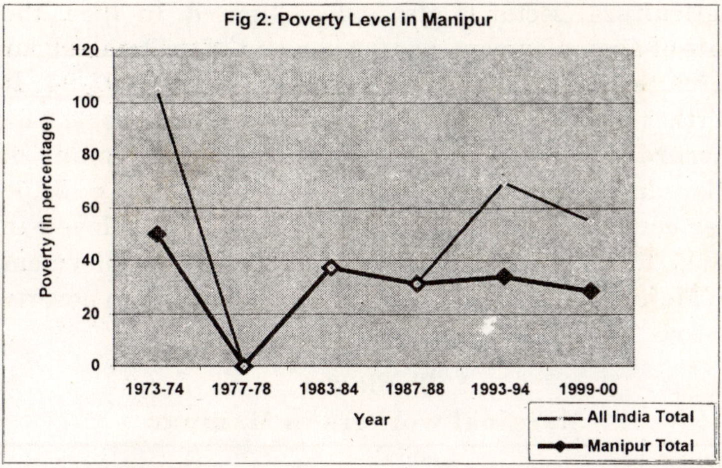

However, statistics show that urban poverty in Manipur is much below the national level. The growth of marginal workers testifies to the extent of incidence of poverty in the population in any economy. The larger the number of marginal workers (Table 2.4), the greater is the incidence of poverty. In 1981 the number of marginal workers in Manipur was 40,469 which increased to 66,621 in 1991 and to 2,85,849 in 2001. In other words, during 1991-2001, the growth rate of marginal workers was 329.06 per cent. Furthermore, the structure and character of economy is largely reflected in the occupational composition. In 2001 in Manipur, workforce engaged in the agricultural activities accounted for 57.37 per cent of the main workers, including 11.31 of agricultural labourers, indicating the continuing marked importance of land-based primary activities, while 9.15 per cent were household industrial workers and 33.46 per cent constituted other workers (Table 2.5). The range of employment opportunity in the agricultural sector is also indeed limited. In 1981, the rate of unemployment was 0.4 per cent of the total labour force, which increased to 1.8 per cent in 1993-94. It further increased to 3.5 per cent in 1999-2000 (Table 2.6). According to the statistics of the Department of Planning, Government of Manipur, 4.93 lakh i.e. 21.58 per cent of the total population were unemployed in 2005. Rural poverty and the incidence of unemployment in Manipur are, therefore, fairly high, but urban poverty is low.

Table 2.4
Marginal workers in Manipur

Year	*Number of marginal workers*	*Percentage*	
		Male	*Female*
1981	40,469	15.32	84.67
1991	66,621	15.0	85.0
2001	2,85,849	34.0	66.0

Source: Government of Manipur, Directorate of Economics and Statistics

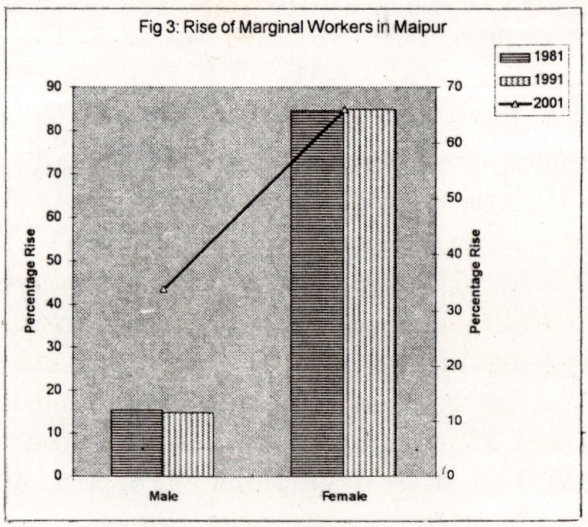

Table 2.5
Distribution of population according to occupation, 2001

Category	*Number of workers*	*Percentage to the total*
Cultivators	4,92,696	46.06
Agri labourers	1,20,991	11.31
Household industry	97,955	9.15
Other workers	3,57,936	33.46

Source: Census Report

Table 2.6
Incidence of unemployment in Manipur (As percentage of labour force)

Year	*Male*	*Female*	*Total*
1981	0.6	0.0	0.4
1991	2.2	1.0	1.82
2001	3.7	3.1	3.5

Source: Rounds of the NSSO (Quoted by the National Human Development Report, 2001)

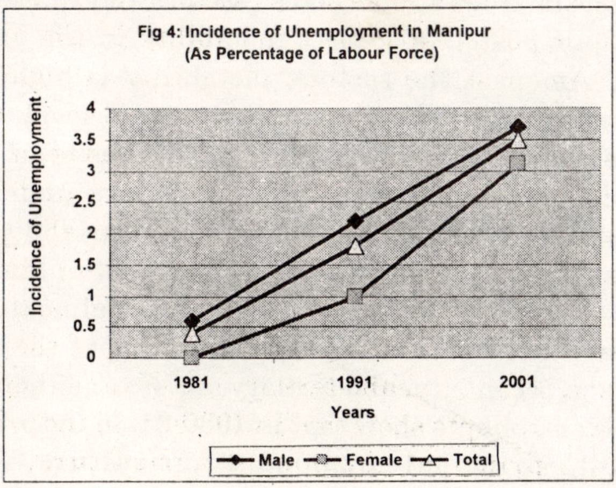

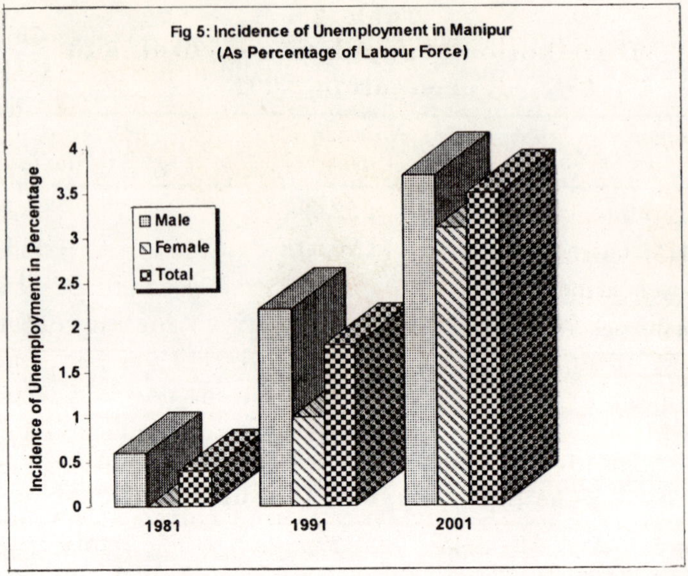

A look at the sectoral composition in the state becomes rather necessary here (Table 2.7 & 2.8). Sectoral growth in Manipur has been volatile over the decades. Variations in growth rates across sectors and sub-sectors in Manipur post-1990 reflect instability in the growth process. Amongst the sectors, instability is highest in the primary sector. Unlike at the national level where inconsistency in secondary sector growth has been much lower, in Manipur almost all sub-sectors under the secondary sector reveal a high degree of variability. On a similar plane, the tertiary sector's growth in Manipur also appears to be unstable. A sectoral delineation of the gross state domestic product, in terms of the share of primary, secondary, and tertiary sectors and their sub-sectoral components show that in 1980-81, in the primary sector, its principal component agriculture, which contributed the largest share of 45.46 per cent, even more than the national average of 44.4 per cent, declined to 29.57 per cent in 2001-02. But this was in conformity with the national trend. The second segment to grow is found to be the unregistered manufacturing activity, a trend supported by historical factors. However, the tertiary sector, which contributed 42.65 per cent, much higher than the all India contribution of 36.45 per cent in 1980-81, saw a rather slow shift of 4.68 per cent to 47.33 in 2001-02 as compared to the all India growth increment of 19.23 per cent during the period 1980-81 to 2001-02. This can be accounted for by the discernible structural differences between the state's economy and that of the national one. The reliance of Manipur on the primary sector in terms of employment at 70 per cent in 1991 was much higher than in terms of income of 35.49 per cent in 1993-94. One finds a contrasting picture in the secondary sector - the share of income originating in this sector was 18.61 per cent in 1993-94, the share of employment was much less at 9.66 per cent.

A high pace of population growth carves down the benefits of growth in terms of per capita income. This is quite evident from the Tables given. The rate of population growth in the state has been substantially higher than the national level, more so in the 1990s than in the 1980s. Whereas at the national level the trend has been towards a declining population growth rate, in case of Manipur it has been just the reverse. Therefore, the advantage in terms of a slightly higher growth rate of Manipur's economy over that at the national level falls off with Manipur's high population growth.

Manipur has also failed in providing infrastructural facilities conducive to social and economic development

Table 2.7

Percentage share and change in percentage share in GSDP/GDP in Manipur and India

(At current prices)

Industries	*Percentage Share*						*Change in Percentages*					
	1980-81		*1993-94*		*2001-02*		*1980-81 to 1993-94*		*1993-94 to 2001-02*		*1981-2002*	
	Manipur	*India*	*Manipur*	*India*	*Manipur*	*India*	*Manipur*	*India*	*Manipur*	*India*	*Manipur*	*India*
	1	*2*	*3*	*4*	*5*	*6*	*7*	*8*	*9*	*10*	*11*	*12*
Agriculture	41.98	35.42	29.18	28.39	22.76	22.62	-12.80	-7.03	-6.42	-12.80	-19.22	-19.82
Forestry & logging	2.22	2.52	3.23	1.47	4.62	1.16	1.01	-1.05	1.40	-1.35	2.41	-2.41
Fishing	1.26	0.74	3.08	1.11	2.18	1.17	1.82	0.37	-0.90	0.43	0.92	0.80
Mining & quarrying	-	1.76	0.00	2.57	0.00	2.29	0.00	0.81	0.00	0.53	0.00	1.34
Primary	**45.46**	**40.44**	**35.49**	**33.54**	**29.57**	**27.25**	**-9.97**	**-6.90**	**-5.92**	**-13.19**	**-15.89**	**-20.09**
Manufacturing	4.75	16.70	0.57	16.06	0.10	15.31	-4.18	-0.64	-0.47	-1.38	-4.65	-2.02

(Contd...)

	1	2	3	4	5	6	7	8	9	10	11	12
Registered	0.29	9.52	0.28	10.48	0.05	10.08	-0.01	0.96	-0.23	0.56	-0.24	1.52
Unregistered	4.46	7.18	7.15	5.58	8.35	5.23	2.70	-1.60	1.20	-1.95	3.90	-3.54
Construction	6.31	4.79	6.68	5.20	10.72	5.95	0.38	0.40	4.04	1.16	4.41	1.56
Elect. gas & water supply	0.84	1.62	4.49	2.43	3.98	2.12	3.65	0.81	-0.51	0.51	3.14	1.32
Secondary	**11.89**	**23.11**	**18.61**	**23.69**	**23.10**	**23.39**	**6.72**	**0.58**	**4.49**	**0.28**	**11.21**	**0.86**
Transport, storage & Communi-cation	1.95	4.49	4.34	6.54	3.81	7.53	2.39	2.05	-0.53	3.03	1.87	5.08
Transport by other means	1.72	2.92	3.70	4.02	3.23	4.92	1.98	1.11	-0.47	2.00	1.51	3.11
Railways	0.01	0.86	0.00	1.23	0.00	0.93	0.00	0.37	0.00	0.07	-0.01	0.44
Communi-cation	0.23	0.61	0.64	1.21	0.58	1.61	0.41	0.60	-0.06	1.00	0.36	1.60

(Contd...)

	1	*2*	*3*	*4*	*5*	*6*	*7*	*8*	*9*	*10*	*11*	*12*
Trade, hotels and restaurants (excluding trade for all India)	5.06	0.68	10.97	0.79	8.44	1.02	5.91	0.11	-2.54	0.34	3.37	0.45
Banking and insurance	1.13	2.97	1.48	5.33	1.10	6.40	0.34	2.36	-0.38	3.43	-0.04	5.79
Real-estate, ownership of dwellings and business services	12.48	6.08	3.94	6.20	2.94	6.53	-8.54	0.11	-1.00	0.45	-9.54	0.56
Public administration	10.26	5.11	13.94	5.58	15.05	6.35	3.68	0.48	1.10	1.25	4.78	1.73
Other services	11.75	6.29	11.23	6.40	16.00	8.23	-0.53	0.11	4.78	1.94	4.25	2.05
Tertiary	**42.65**	**36.45**	**45.90**	**42.77**	**47.33**	**49.36**	**3.25**	**6.32**	**1.43**	**12.91**	**4.68**	**19.23**
Gross Domestic Product	**100**	**100**	**100**	**100**	**100**	**100**						

Source: Statistical Abstract, Manipur, Various Years

Table 2.8
Average annual growth rate of (GSDP) in Manipur & average annual growth rate (GDP)

Industries	*Average annual growth rate 1980-81 to 1993-94 (1980-81 prices)*		*Average annual rate growth 1993-94 to 2001-02 (1993-94 prices)*		*Change in growth rate*	
	Manipur	*India*	*Manipur*	*India*	*Manipur*	*India*
	1	*2*	*3*	*4*	*5*	*6*
Agriculture	1.97	3.62	2.28	3.04	0.31	-0.58
Forestry & logging	4.47	-0.16	11.26	1.84	6.79	2.00
Fishing	16.17	6.42	7.06	4.36	-9.11	-2.06
Mining & quarrying	-	7.03	-	4.54	-	-2.49
Primary	**2.75**	**3.58**	**3.34**	**3.13**	**0.58**	**-0.45**
Manufacturing	3.13	6.34	11.60	6.95	8.47	0.61
Registered	30.90	7.45	-8.28	7.09	-39.18	-0.36
Unregistered	3.05	4.73	12.16	6.73	9.11	2.00
Construction	7.07	4.47	14.35	6.00	7.29	1.53
Electricity, gas & water supply	28.47	8.48	6.30	6.20	-22.17	-2.27

(Contd...)

	1	*2*	*3*	*4*	*5*	*6*
Secondary	**4.88**	**5.76**	**10.45**	**6.65**	**5.57**	**0.89**
Transport, storage & Communication	17.06	6.25	6.07	9.65	-10.99	3.40
Transport by other means	17.90	6.62	5.13	6.99	-12.77	0.37
Railways	-	4.47	-	4.88	-	0.40
Storage	0.00	3.60	0.42	1.71	0.42	-1.89
Communication	11.22	7.72	10.83	19.13	-0.3	11.42
Trade, hotels and restaurants (excluding trade for India)	3.71	7.04	5.45	10.75	1.74	3.72
Banking & Insurance	9.36	13.04	7.64	8.92	-1.72	-4.12
Real estate, ownership of dwellings and business	5.08	9.07	4.92	5.81	-0.16	-3.26
Public administration	6.95	6.44	8.70	6.97	1.74	0.53
Other services	6.92	6.03	12.28	8.55	5.37	2.51
Tertiary	**6.89**	**6.55**	**7.79**	**8.15**	**0.90**	**1.60**
Gross State Domestic Product	**4.95**	**5.99**	**6.72**	**6.24**	**1.77**	**0.25**

Source: Statistical Abstract, Manipur, Various Years

of the state. According to the XIth Finance Commission, Manipur's index of economic and social infrastructure was 75.39. Among the North Eastern states only Tripura (74.87) and Arunachal Pradesh (69.71) had indices lower than that of Manipur. The CMIE index of relative development of infrastructure too shows that Manipur lags behind the national average by a one-fifth.

In 2002-03, the per capita consumption of electricity in Manipur was 72.21 Kwh (Table 2.9). The average level is dismally low and is reflected in the slow pace of industrialization in the state. Taking all the demand for electricity into account, the 16th Electric Power Survey of India assessed the year-wise demand for electrical energy and power in Manipur since 1999. It shows that the state is unable to meet an increasing proportion of its energy requirement each year, and as a result the power deficit in the state has been growing continually over the last six years. No doubt, the gap between Manipur and the all-India average has been ever widening.

Road-connectivity in Manipur vis-à-vis the other states of the region and the all-India level in terms of both, density and quality is quite poor (Table 2.10 & 2.11). The road density per 100 Sq. km. is only 51.2 as against all-India figure of 77. The road length per 100 sq. km and the percentage of surfaced roads for Manipur are far below the all-India average - a fact pointed out way back in 1963 still holds. The Manipur State Transport (MST) established in 1945 has also been a failure. Unable to sustain losses over a period of time, yielding a negative return on investment, with its functions having been entirely taken over by private operators, the MST Corporation today exists only in name. Growth of communication sector too fares no better. Railways, which are the cheapest form of travel, have only a token presence of 1.5 km in the state. Inland water-ways are practically nonexistent, even though at one time the small rivers criss-crossing the valley was used for transporting goods and people by boats. Transportation is therefore very much road-based in Manipur. Roadways remain the lifeline and serve for foundation for economic development in the state. The development tempo of the state largely depends upon the conditions of the 434 km of National Highways (NH53 and NH39) and the 1436.94 km of State Roadways (No 31). Still appalling has been the growth of the telecommunication infrastructure (Table 2.12).

Table 2.9
Growth of per capita consumption of electricity in Manipur

Year	*Installed capacity in Kw*	*Per capita consumption of electricity in Kwh*	
		Manipur	*India*
1972-73	7600	-	-
1980-81	20779	7.68	135
1984-85	24270	34.00	167
1989-90	12070	98.00	236
1995-96	12371	120.00	-
1999-00	11845	77.00	354.70
2002-03	47252	72.21	-

Source: Chief Engineer, Power, Government of Manipur, Statistical Handbook of Manipur 2002, Directorate of Economics & Statistics Government of Manipur Imphal.

Table 2.10
Comparative road statistics: NER (as on 31st March, 1997)

State	*Road length per 100 sq.Km*	*% of surfaced road to total road length*
Arunachal Pradesh	16.80	28.32
Assam	87.20	16.94
Manipur	49.00	32.88
Meghalaya	37.80	46.26
Mizoram	22.90	41.10
Nagaland	110.70	26.55
Tripura	140.50	31.10
All India	74.90	58.68

Source: Basic Statistics of Northeastern region (NER) 2002, E&M Cell Government of India, Northeastern Council Secretariat

Table 2.11
Development of roads in Manipur (in km)

As on 31st March	*National Highways*	*State Highways*	*Major District Roads*	*Other District Roads*	*Inter Village Roads*	*Total*
1973	212.30	650.10	574.30	247.90	1029.10	2907.50
1983	434.30	524.00	620.00	332.00	1986.00	4090.10
1993	434.00	1158.00	1010.00	744.00	2428.00	5896.00
1999	957.00	675.00	964.00	1013.00	3563.00	7172.00
2002	957.00	675.00	964.00	1013.00	3563.00	7172.00

Note: * Inclusive of other district and inter village roads
Source: Public Works Department

Table 2.12
Growth of communication sector in Manipur

Year	*No. of post offices*	*No. of combined post & telegraph offices*	*No. of telephones*
1955-56	80	-	-
1960-61	154	6	117
1970-71	252	15	996
1980-81	486	37	2,123
1990-91	605	37	5,026
2000-01	692	47	29,453
2002-03	694	47	41,468

Source: Statistical Handbook of Manipur, Directorate of Economics & Statistics Government of Manipur Imphal, Various Issues & Statistical Abstract of Manipur 2004, Directorate of Economic & Statistics, Government of Manipur.

The data displayed in the tabular forms clearly testifies to the commonly held view that Manipur is one of the low performing states in the country. Taking these hard data, the politically argumentative regional forces tend to harp on that the Centre has kept the state away from its development agenda and allowed it to remain underdeveloped and thus dependent on the Union Government for each and every trifling matter. It is quite natural that during electioneering the developmental issues draw attention of the political parties; while the ruling party tends to highlight its record of achievements in the development of the state, the opposition parties, particularly, the regional ones release a barrage of attack on the government for its failure on all fronts, specially, on the economic ones because of which the state has been reeling under insurgency.

To project underdevelopment and insurgency as two sides of the same coin is a common referral point in discourses on political economy of any of the states in North East India. Manipur is no exception to it. It has been suffering from both. Elections, whether for two Lok Sabha seats or for a 60 member Assembly, provide an opportunity to all the political contestants to place before the electorate their agenda for economic development of the state, and thus, to handle the insurgency related crises, through development and performance. In a subsequent Chapter, it will be revealed how the development issues overshadowed other politically charged ones as election campaigns gathered momentum.

REFERENCES

1. For details about *Lallup* see Jalad Baran Ganguly, *An Economic History of North East India: 1926-1947*(New Delhi: Akansha, 2006), pp. 313-14 and the economy of the state during the pre-Independence period see Chapter 19.
2. *Imperial Gazetteer of Manipur,1909.*
3. Aribam Brajakumar Sharma and Khumujam Ratankumar Singh (eds), *Influx of Migrants into Manipur: A Threat to the Indigenous Ethnic People* (Imphal: United Committee Manipur, 2005).

3

THE PRE-ELECTION HEAT

Politics, in classical perception, is the science of governance of a state, with the prime objective of ensuring welfare of all the citizens. Although there is no universally accepted single definition of the term, it is widely understood as a process in which groups of people participate to take decisions on matters of common interests. Notwithstanding its general applicability to denote the affairs of civil government that operate within the constitutional limits, politics is inextricably associated with all human group interactions. It is a part as well as a craft of management of power, which resides and emanates in the most visible form in all the manifestations of the state, including the use, control and capture of power.

Elections to the seat of power could be treated as the most democratic means to capture power, and therefore, in the political process of a country, it is respected as the cornerstone to legitimize the occupation of offices that are constitutionally created to operate the centers of power. In tune with this definition of election viewed from the prism of popular sovereignty, Montesquieu points out in *The Spirit of*

Laws that at the time of elections people act as "masters" selecting their government "servants".[1]

As already indicated in the preceding Chapter, Manipur has been reeling under the unbearable weight of insurgency, which has torn apart the normal fabric of civic life in the state. Close on the heels of insurgency, there had been political instability since 1967, when the elected government was toppled by defection. Just as insurgency has become a part of the life, floor-crossing and toppling of elected government, one after another, became the order of the day till 2002, when the Congress-led Government was installed with a comfortable and assured viable support. The existence of anti-defection law prevented any disgruntled MLAs from crossing the floor for better and attractive political deals. While the experiments with by now inevitable coalition politics have been successful at the center and in a number of states[2], Manipur presents a case altogether different from the general trend. This peculiarity is due to the self-regarding interests of various legislators, as explained in the preceding Chapter, that disdainfully prevented whatever coalition arrangements had been tried since October 1967 from functioning. Such a situation is the direct outcome of the fluid election trend in the state.

The Election Trend

The first elections in the post-colonial era to the Manipur's representative body, known at that time as the Territorial Council, took place in June-July 1948. It was a historic event, for, it was the first ever election based on universal adult franchise soon after the British had left. The Elections started on June 11 and continued till July 27 owing primarily to communication difficulties and remoteness of certain areas. A ratio of

30:18:3 had been fixed for the representation of general, hill and Muslim constituencies respectively with an additional two seats for the representatives of educational and commercial interests, making Council's total strength 53. The Imphal valley was divided inot 29 constituencies, out of which 3 were plural, where a voter has two votes, one for the Muslim and the other for the non-Muslim candidates. These three special constituencies were Linong, Mayang Imphal and Yiripok, where this arrangement was done to ensure double representation. Moirang constituency also had a similar arrangement of double representation – one hillman was to be elected along with a general candidate. In other words, it was more or less a communal award. It is interesting to note that in the Lilong constituency, both the elected candidates were Muslims. This led to a legal tussle, challenging the election of Md. Alimunddin from the general category. However, the judgment went in his favour.[3]

As stated in Chapter I, Manipur became an integral part of the Indian Union, after the Maharaja had signed the merger document in 1949 and was given the status of a 'C' category state, under Articles 239-24, Part IX of the Constitution. After the merger, the elections to the Electoral College were held in 1952 as per the provisions of the Indian Constitution and on party line. The elections to the 30 member Electoral College, returned 10 from the Congress making it the largest party in the elected body. Table 3.1 shows the party positions in the Electoral College.

The Electoral College was converted into Territorial Council on January 1, 1957 with the same strength. However, with two nominated members, the total strength was raised to 32. Soon after the elevation to a better status, elections were held to the 30-member Territorial Council where no party could secure absolute majority (Table 3.2).

Table 3.1
Party positions in the Electoral College, 1952

Sl.No.	*Parties*	*Seats*
1.	Congress	10
2.	All Manipur National Union	3
3.	Praja Shanti Party	3
4.	Achumba Pamba Congress	2
5.	Kuki National Association	2
6.	CPI	2
7.	Mao Maram Union	2
8.	Manipur Laliangrong Union	2
9.	Gandhi Sewak Sangh	1
10.	Praja Socialist Party	1
11.	Mizo Union	1
12.	Independent	1
13	Total	30

Source: State Election Office, Imphal

Some of the local political parties such as the Paite Union, the Communist Manipur and the Historical Research Society fielded their candidates, but drew a blank.

Table 3.2
Party-wise performance in Territorial Council elections, 1957

Sl. No.	*Parties*	*No. of Seats contested*	*Seat won*	*% of votes polled*
1.	Congress	30	12	28.01
2.	SSP	23	7	19.87
3.	PSP	21	-	5.78
4.	CPI	17	4	11.40
5.	Independents	57	7	34.94
6.	Total	148	30	100.00

Source: State Election Office, Imphal

In the second Territorial Council elections held in 1962, the Congress improved its position securing 15 out of the 30 seats increasing its tally by 3 (Table 3.3). It also improved its support base by polling 29.15 per cent of the votes, 1.01 per cent more than the previous one. It snatched one seat from the Socialists and two from the CPI.

Table 3.3
Party-wise performance in Territorial Council elections, 1962

Sl. No.	*Party*	*Seats contested*	*Seats won*	*PC of votes polled*	*% in Seats contested*
1	Congress	29	15	29.15	32.70
2	SSP	27	5	19.44	27.73
3	CPI	14	0	7.13	23.95
4	PSP	12	0	2.99	3.93
5	Independents	92	10	41.29	48.85
6	Total	174	30	100	

Source: State Election Office, Imphal

The Independents backed by various social groups, including the secessionist elements, secured 41.29 percentage of votes polled. They played the most crucial role in formation of the government, headed by M. Koireng Singh. Both the CPI and the PSP were routed in the elections. The Socialists could, however, manage to retain 5 out of its 7 seats.

The Territorial Council was upgraded to a Territorial Assembly in July 1963, with the same composition of 30 elected and 2 nominated members, thus adding some respectability to this elected body.

The first Territorial Assembly elections were held in the early part of 1967. People's enthusiasm was quite visible. As many as 156 contestants – all were male as in the past - were in the fray for the 30 member Assembly. The polling percentage was also high with 69.10%. in which the Congress faired well. It improved its tally from by one seat out of 28 seats contested (Table 3.4) and polled 32.53 per cent votes, which is a significant increase by 3.38 per cent. The Socialists too improved their voting share but had to concede one seat in favour of the CPI. The CPI(M) contested for the first time in this election after the split of the CPI in 1962. The independents once again improved the share in the percentage of voting despite the loss of one seat to the Congress. The increase in the votes polled by the Independents eventually had a role to play in the regional politics in Manipur.

Table 3.4
Party-wise performance in the Territorial Assembly elections, 1967

Sl. No.	*Party*	*Seats contested*	*Seats won*	*PC of votes polled*	*% of votes in seats contested*
1	Congress	29	16	32.53	32.70
2	SSP	12	4	11.70	27.73
3	CPI	6	1	5.47	23.95
4	CPI(M)	5	0	0.67	3.41
5	PSP	5	0	0.77	3.93
6	Independents	99	9	48.86	48.86
7	Total	156	30	100	

Source: Election Commission of India

The trend remained without dramatic change with incremental electoral fortune for the Congress as it could register success in increasing its seats in the elected body and also in its support base in the state. The Socialists could improve their support base in terms of percentage of votes polled but had to lose one seat in the Assembly. The Independents' success in terms of increasing their support base by 7.57 despite the loss of one merits consideration in view of their role in the process of ministry formation and eventually in engineering defection leading to toppling it in no time. The trend, as already stated in the preceding Chapter, was set in the developments following the 1967 elections.

In 1972, as already indicated, the status of statehood was conferred upon Manipur, 23 years of its formal merger. Along with the historic event, the Territorial Assembly was renamed as Legislative Assembly with 60 elected members. The new arrangement led to the redrawing of constituencies – 40 in the valley and 20 in the hill areas. It was a remarkable, though belated, milestone in the political development in the state of Manipur. A new regional political party called the Manipur People's Party (MPP) entered the political scene of the state, so also Bharatiya Jan Sangh entered the election politics in the state for the first time.

The one party domination in Manipur politics came to an end after the 1972 Assembly elections. The Congress party was already riddled with factionalism and defection[4] leading to the fall of the Ministry. The intra-party conflict was reflected in the election results. The party suffered loss in the election in the wake of the resurgence of the regional party politics and the readjustment of constituencies, which had experienced

100 per cent increase. It could capture only 17 seats and the percentage of votes polled in its favour came down to 30.02 which amounts to a loss of 2.51 per cent. The MPP secured 15 out of 42 seats contested, polled 20.17 per cent votes, and thus, captured 25 per cent of the strength in the Assembly, but was short of 16 to form the government. Md. Alimuddin, Congressman, switched his allegiance to the MPP and became the Chief Minister with the support of the Independents, the MHU and the KNA. In terms of the percentage of votes the Independents faired will securing 18.79 per cent of votes and won 5 seats (Table 3.5). The only woman candidate Aribam Bimola Devi contested from Kontha under the banner of MPP could poll only 1301 votes and was thus defeated. She was the first woman candidate who broke the jinx of gender alienation in the electoral process in Manipur.

Table 3.5

Party-wise performance in the Assembly elections, 1972

Sl. No.	*Party*	*Seats contested*	*Seats won*	*PC of votes polled*	*% of votes in seats contested*
1	Congress	60	17	30.02	30.02
2	Congress (O)	10	1	2.37	13.96
3	CPI	25	5	10.13	22.54
4	CPI(M)	5	0	0.66	7.51
5	MPP	42	15	20.17	27.75
6	SSP	16	3	5.35	18.76
7	MHU	16	12	9.57	NA
8	KNA	6	2	2.94	NA
9	Independents	82	5	18.79	18.79
10	Total	262	60	100	

Source: Election Commission of India and State Election Office, Imphal

Politics of defection and toppling of ministries that plagued the political scenario of Manipur had started soon after the 1967 elections. Thus followed the unwarranted mid-term elections. The first one of this variety took place in 1974 in which the MPP became the single largest party in the Assembly with 15 seats (Table 3.6), still short of 16 members to have an absolute majority in the house of 60. There were allegations of horse-trading which led to the formation of the MPP-led ministry. The story continues to dominate the political scenario till 2002.

Table 3.6
Party-wise performance in the Assembly elections, 1974

Sl. No.	*Party*	*Seats contested*	*Seats won*	*PC of votes polled*	*% of votes in seats contested*
1	Congress	49	13	27.62	33.32
2	CPI	12	6	5.54	28.95
3	CPI (M)	3	0	0.56	11.17
4	Congress (o)	14	0	1.47	6.48
5	SSP	18	2	5.93	19.50
6	MPP	40	20	22.55	34.35
7	KNA	6	2	2.95	25.79
8	MHU	16	12	9.36	34.12
9	Independents	107	5	24.02	33.05
10	Total	265	60	100	

Source: Election Commission of India

Three women contested in the 1974 Assembly elections. None could win. Aribam Bimola Devi changed her constituency and decided to contest from Heingang with the MPP ticket but was defeated. She could improve her performance by increasing 1558 votes. The other candidates were T. Kholly (Independent) and Lhingjaneng (Congress) who were defeated by a margin of 655 and 1124 votes respectively.

In the 1980 elections new political parties joined the fray. The Janata Party, the Janata Party (JP) and the Janata Party (Secular) contested the election without however making any impact (Table 3.7). The Congress base eroded alarmingly. The MHU did not field any candidate after tasting uncomfortable defeat in previous elections. The Independents once again held the key in the process of ministry formation, as they constituted the largest segment in the Assembly followed by the Congress. They also polled the highest percentage of votes.

Table 3.7

Party-wise performance in the Assembly elections, 1980

Sl. No.	*Party*	*Seats contested*	*Seats won*	*PC of votes polled*	*% of votes in seats contested*
1	Congress	58	13	21.63	22.35
2	Congress (U)	40	6	9.48	14.59
3	CPI	23	5	7.29	19.47
4	CPI (M)	2	1	0.57	18.30
5	Janta Party	56	10	19.71	20.97
6	Janta Party (JP)	1	0	0.13	8.16

(Contd...)

Sl. No.	Party	Seats contested	Seats won	PC of votes polled	% of votes in seats contested
7	Janta Party (Secular)	15	0	2.83	10.90
8	KNA	7	2	2.82	21.36
9	MPP	40	4	6.59	10.01
10	Independent	159	19	28.98	33.60
11	Total	401	60	100	

Source: Election Commission of India

Seven women candidates belonging to different political parties secured nominations to contest from seven constituencies. This time the attempt was serious, for, there was only one woman candidate in each of the seven constituencies so that the votes were not divided. Yet none was elected. T. Kholly (Independent contesting from Saikot ST constituency) secured 3719 votes, which accounts for 21.41 per cent of votes, the highest among all the women candidates.

Manipur once again had mid-term poll in 1984. This time there were two additions to the national party, the Lok Dal, joining the elections politics and the other was the splinter Indian National Congress (Socialist). As in the past, none could reach double digit (Table 3.8).

After a long wait of 17 years the Congress could secure half of the seats, while the MPP could retain only 3 seats. As in the past, the Independents once again secured one third of the seats in the Assembly. The Congress could form the government with the support of Independents. This time five women contested and none of them could win. All of them forfeited their security deposits.

Table 3.8
Party-wise performance in the Assembly elections, 1984

Sl. No.	*Party*	*Seats contested*	*Seats won*	*PC of votes polled*	*% of votes in seats contested*
1	BJP	12	0	0.71	3.89
2	CPI	17	1	4.15	15.63
3	CPI (M)	2	0	0.09	3.39
4	Congress	60	30	29.82	29.82
5	Congress (S)	19	0	3.26	10.32
6	Janata Party	21	4	6.08	18.06
7	Lok Dal	2	0	0.42	12.32
8	KNA	4	1	1.55	19.93
9	MPP	34	3	10.81	19.19
10	Independents	193	21	43.12	47.32
11	Total	364	60	100	

Source: Election Commission of India

In the 1990 elections, polls could not be held in 6 constituencies, owing to insurgency related troubles. The polling took place in 54 constituencies, and the voter turnout was 89.95 per cent, which was definitely impressive. The combined regional parties (the MPP, the KNA and newly formed MHPC, and the NPP) could improve their positions, securing 12 seats. The strength of the Congress in the Assembly was reduced to 24, despite its better performance in terms of votes polled

(33.71%). It needed the support of 4 legislators to form the government. This time there was no role for the Independents to fill the vacuum, as they could not score electoral victory in any of the constituencies (Table 3.9)

Table 3.9
Party-wise performance in the Assembly election, 1990

Sl. No.	*Party*	*Seats contested*	*Seats won*	*PC of votes polled*	*% of votes in seats contested*
1	BJP	11	0	1.87	10.11
2	CPI	13	3	4.14	17.94
3	Congress (S)	31	4	12.41	20.75
4	Congress	54	24	33.71	33.71
5	Janata Dal	46	11	19.82	23.17
6	KNA	8	2	2.62	15.42
7	MPP	41	9	19.41	25.46
8	MHPC	10	0	0.89	4.46
9	NPP	5	1	0.78	9.38
10	Independents	35	0	4.35	12.40
11	Total	254	54	100	

Source: Election Commission of India

The 1990 elections will be remembered as a historic one for electing a woman candidate, out of seven in the fray. She was Hangmi Shaiza, a Tangkhul Naga by birth, from the Ukhrul constituency, which is predominantly inhabited by the Tangkhul Naga community. It is the place of birth of the NSCN leader, T. Muivah. It is, therefore, known as the stronghold of NSCN (IM).

Hangmi Shaiza, the wife of the slain former Chief Minister for two stints, (from July to December 1974 and June 1977 to November 1979), Yangmaso Shaiza, was a school teacher, and had been associated with a number of civil society organizations and represented India at All Asia Women Conference in 1967. She contested on a Janata Dal ticket and secured 7922 votes (44.36%). The constituency was earlier held by an Independent, A.S. Arthur. It is noteworthy that Shaiza gave up politics and inducted her son Denny who has been representing the constituency since 2000, first as a BJP candidate for two occasions (2000 and 2002) and now as a UNC supported Independent candidate.

The 1995 elections witnessed a rally of seven regional parties having of course, different agenda. Except the MPP, none could enlist the support of the electorate (Table 3.10). The MPP could secure 23.67 per cent votes and capture 18 seats in the Assembly and thus was placed next to the Congress, which had a tally of 22 members. Although 11 women contested in the election, victory eluded them. Hangmi Shaiza, the sitting MLA and the first woman legislator, decided not to contest the election in order to accommodate her son Denny Shaiza, who, however, could not win.

The Assembly poll of 2000 did not show any sign of improvement in the political situation. The same story of hung Assembly was repeated. The MSCP captured 23 seats, which was the highest, followed by the Congress with 11 (Table 3.11). Under the fluid situation, W. Nipamacha Singh once again became the Chief Minister for slightly more than a year. There was no let up in the instability caused by shifting allegiance; Radhabinod Koijam staged a dramatic capture of power, overthrowing Nipamacha Singh. He, however, could enjoy power for hardly four months. The ministry collapsed, forcing mid-term elections in 2002. A record number of 14 women contested the elections in 2000, but only one named Wahengbam Leima Devi (Independent) was elected from the Naoriya Pakhanglakpa constituency.

Table 3.10
Party-wise performance in the Assembly elections, 1995

Sl. No.	*Party*	*Seats contested*	*Seats won*	*PC of votes polled*	*% of votes in seats contested*
1	BJP	20	1	3.35	10.82
2	CPI	23	2	5.59	15.49
3	CPI (M)	2	0	0.20	6.44
4	Congress	60	22	28.65	28.65
5	Janata Dal	40	7	11.92	18.19
6	Janata Party	4	0	0.14	1.73
7	SAP	23	2	6.19	15.57
8	Congress (S)	13	1	3.91	16.06
9	KNA	6	0	0.25	2.32
10	MPP	55	18	23.67	26.59
11	FPM	22	2	4.91	13.62
12	MHPC	1	0	0.21	10.61
13	NPP	5	2	2.65	26.26
14	SJP	6	0	0.63	6.09
15	Independents	67	3	7.73	12.45
16	Total	347	60	100	

Source: Election Commission of India

Table 3.11
Party-wise performance in the Assembly elections, 2000

Sl. No.	*Party*	*Seats contested*	*Seats won*	*PC of votes polled*	*% of votes in seats contested*
1	BJP	39	6	11.28	18.32
2	CPI	15	0	3.60	14.33
3	CPI (M)	4	0	0.30	5.44
4	Congress	47	11	18.31	22.94
5	Janata Dal (S)	8	1	1.58	12.88
6	Janata Dal (U)	18	1	1.79	5.98
7	NCP	41	5	7.87	11.51
8	FPM	39	6	9.44	13.76
9	MPP	29	4	7.90	16.45
10	MSCP	57	23	26.28	27.36
11	RJD	15	1	1.83	7.54
12	RSP	3	0	0.08	1.08
13	SP	36	1	6.68	10.58
14	KNA	1	0	0.05	2.17
15	NPP	1	0	0.00	0.05
16	Independents	48	1	3.01	7.44
17	Total	401	60	100	

Source: Election Commission of India.

In the 2002 elections, only two parties, the Congress and the FPM, attained the two-digit mark in number of seats in the Assembly. While the Congress captured 20, the FPM could raise its tally to 13, a definite improvement upon its performance, two years back (Table 3.12). The Congress being the single largest party was invited to form the government, with the support of other parties. Okram Ibobi Singh managed to lead a stable government, in spite of minor occasional hiccups. It completed the tenure of five years without facing any major threat, a remarkable feat since 1967.

Table 3.12
Party-wise performance in the Assembly elections, 2002

Sl. No.	*Party*	*Seats contested*	*Seats won*	*PC of votes polled*	*% of votes in seats contested*
1	BJP	46	4	9.55	12.11
2	CPI	16	5	4.40	18.40
3	CPI(M)	1	0	0.03	2.03
4	Congress	58	20	26.18	27.62
5	NCP	33	3	9.44	17.10
6	FPM	48	13	18.14	22.96
7	MPP	14	2	3.03	12.85
8	MSCP	42	7	12.40	18.27
9	SAP	31	3	8.33	15.06
10	Janata Dal (U)	7	0	0.16	1.39
11	DRPP	23	2	3.93	11.39
12	LS	3	0	0.00	0.05
13	MNC	23	1	4.03	10.36
14	NNLP	5	0	0.05	0.40
15	SJP	1	0	0.01	0.96
16	Independents	17	0	0.33	1.81
17	Total	368	60	100	

Source: Election Commission of India

There were 7 women contesting the 2002 elections and out of them only Wahengbam Leima Devi, the sitting Independent MLA, who had joined the Congress before the elections, could retain her seat. Five others forfeited their deposits.

The data displayed in all the Tables reveal the trend in the election politics in Manipur. Except the Congress, none of the national parties could make a breakthrough in the elections held so far. It clearly shows the weakness of the non-Congress parties, as also the political hold of the Congress among the electorate. The figures shown in Table 3.13 is a testimony to the aforesaid conclusion.

The most striking aspect of the election trend in Manipur is the low polling in favour of the regional parties. Except for a transitional wave in support to regionalism when the MPP secured 19.40 and 23.67 votes respectively in 1990 and 1995, all the regional parties failed miserably in the electoral struggle. The MSCP's performance in 2000 was not unexpected, as it was an off-shoot of the Congress which could not manage the internal bickering over leadership and power sharing. The FPM's performance in 2002 was a temporary feature, for, it could not sustain its support base in the 2007. The Congress, on the other hand, had been performing better than regional parties. Only in 2000, it secured record low of 18.31 per cent votes. The ups and downs of the Congress is reflective of its national trend. Despite the upbeat mood of regionalism, one has to note that various shades of regionalism, such as linguistic, geographical and ethnic affiliations divide the share of votes. The MPP, which had registered a statistically significant emergence in 1972, suffered erosion in its support base in the next general elections in the wake of internal

Table 3.13

Percentage of votes polled by major parties in Manipur elections 1952-2002

Parties	*1967*	*1972*	*1974*	*1980*	*1984*	*1990*	*1995*	*2000*	*2002*
JS/BJP	-	0.22	-	-	0.71	1.87	3.35	11.28	9.55
CPI	5.47	10.13	5.54	7.26	4.15	4.14	5.59	3.60	4.40
CPI(M)	0.67	0.66	0.56	0.57	0.09	-	0.20	0.30	0.03
Congress	32.53	30.02	27.62	21.63	29.82	33.71	28.65	18.31	26.18
MPP		20.17	22.55	6.59	10.81	19.40	23.67	7.90	3.03
KNA			2.95	2.82	1.55	2.61	0.25	0.05	-
MSCP								26.28	12.40
FPM								9.44	18.14
Independents	48.85	31.08	24.02	28.98	43.12	4.35	7.73	3.01	0.33

Source: Election Commission of India

dissentions and emergence of ethnicity-based new parties such as the KNA and the FPM. The voters had their choices in the politics of regionalism, while the Congress had a solid support base strong enough to withstand any transitional assault.

The putative assumption that the state has a deep-rooted regional sentiment is a myth. Another significant trend is that being aware of the politics of horse-trading, which had been afflicting the state politics of Manipur for long, the electorate had started gradually rejecting the Independent candidates. While the Congress had been the frontrunner in all the elections, securing the highest number of seats in the Assembly, other national parties are yet to make a mark. The BJP could register some success in 2002, by securing 11.28 per cent votes, but suffered a loss in two years time; it is yet to recover from that loss. The CPI used to contest in all the elections but it's performance is far from satisfactory. The CPI (M) has always drawn a blank ever since it entered the election fray in 1967, and never polled even 1 per cent of votes.

It is interesting to note that in the land of the Meira Paibies, where the women come out to vote in large numbers with the past successive elections witnessing their larger share in votes, they have failed miserably in the election politics. In the patriarchal society of Manipur, it was in 1972 only a woman candidate Aribam Bimola Devi got a ticket from the MPP to contest from the Kontha Assembly constituency. She secured 1302 votes which accounted for 20.22 per cent of the valid votes polled. This marked the beginning of women participation in the Assembly elections. Manipuri women have a long road to traverse before they have an adequate share in the election politics of the state (Table 3.14).

Table 3.14
Number of women contesting Assembly elections 1972-2002

Year	*Number*	*Winner*
1972	1	0
1974	3	0
1980	7	0
1984	5	0
1990	7	1
1995	11	0
2000	14	1
2002	7	1

Source: Election Commission of India

Hangmi Shaiza won the election because of sympathy vote, despite the fact that she had been associated with a number of civil society organizations. As already stated, her husband Yangmaso Shaiza, former Chief Minister of Manipur for two stints, was killed by militants on January 30, 1984. In most of other cases, the contestants forfeited their security deposit.

As already stated, women used to cast vote in large numbers. In all the Assembly elections since 1984, the percentage of turnout of woman voters, barring the elections of 2000, exceeded that of the male ones (Table 3.15). Two factors determine the large turn out of woman voters. The presence of women in all walks of life is widely seen throughout the length and breadth of the state; with the air of festivity on the day of the poll, women would like to make their presence felt with their best attire. Second, they are prone to be influenced by the male members of the family to cast vote in favour of candidates of the latters' choice, in which the female members have the least say.

Table 3.15
Male-female turnout in percentage in the Assembly elections 1967-2002

Year	*Male*	*Female*	*Total*
1967	70.23	67.99	69.10
1972	78.41	73.52	75.89
1974	84.40	84.80	84.60
1980	85.12	79.91	82.42
1984	85.66	88.94	87.29
1990	89.33	90.57	89.95
1995	90.87	91.95	91.41
2000	89.99	89.75	89.87
2002	90.27	90.49	90.38

Source: Election Commission of India

Table 3.15 is a clear testimony to not only the people's participation in the elections but also their allegiance to the Constitution of the country. Dissatisfaction, expressed through demonstrations of various kinds with the Union Government on certain vital issues, like withdrawal of the AFSPA and the high handedness of the security forces on innocent civilians, could not be linked up with secessionism spearheaded by certain sections of the society. That is why each time, a boycott call given by the militants had been responded to by the people in participating in the election in a resounding manner, far surpassing the national fervour.

Announcement of the elections and speculations

The Election Commission of India announced the 9th Assembly elections in Manipur on December 29, 2006.[5] Before the dates of the elections were announced there had been a speculation that most of the militant groups would boycott the elections and force others to do so. Such a situation would have definitely marred the entire election process. It was nothing new to issue a call for the boycott, but each and every boycott call was emphatically answered by high voter turnout with few exceptions that could be seen only in insurgent-dominant remote areas. The speculations were rife that there would be call for boycott, as in the past, centering around the demand for the withdrawal of the AFSPA; tagged to it would be the Naga militants' demand for a greater Nagalim, which seeks to include a substantial territorial area of Manipur. As the dates of elections were announced – February 8, 14 and 23, 2007 – with the three-phased elections notified, the fear of boycott call was supplanted by a call not to support national parties. The call was flashed in most of the local dailies. The Congress candidates were being 'threatened' by banned militant groups to either stay out of the poll process or pay money. Amidst reports of this kind, the Congress President Sonia Gandhi came to Manipur for campaigning to instil courage and confidence in the minds of the candidates.[6]

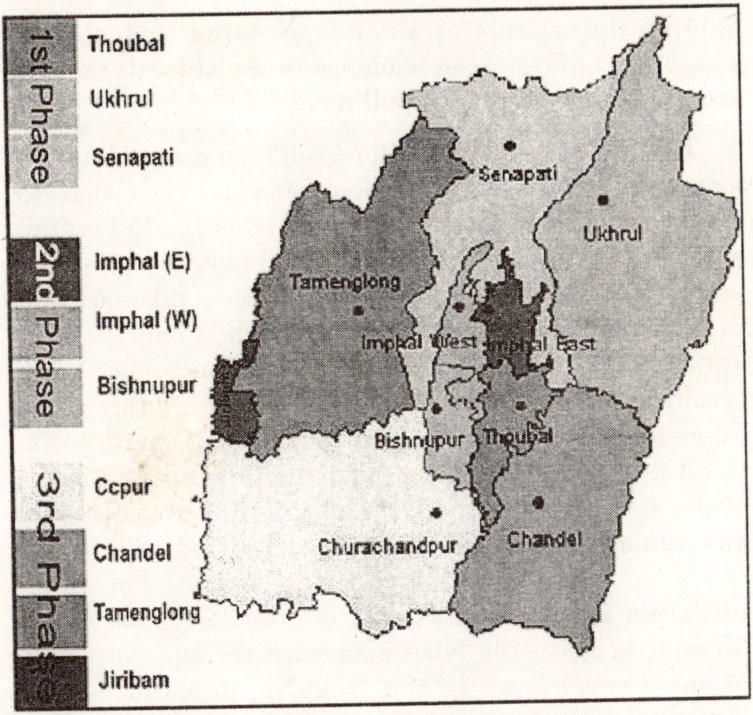

Map showing the areas scheduled for three-phased Assembly election

Manipur has a history of election boycott calls issued by insurgent groups; but interestingly enough, the overwhelming majority had invariably ignored these fully and substantially. Therefore, this time, instead of making a repetition of the same fruitless exercise, the militants gave a call to boycott national parties. No one gave credence to this slightly different call. As many as 5 national parties, 8 state parties, 5 unrecognized but registered parties besides 55 Independents, and in all 308 candidates, contested the elections. The UNC itself fielding its candidates as Independents, reduced the possibility of large-scale violence in the state during the campaign period and on poll days.

The speculation that the Congress might improve its tally seemed brighter for four reasons. The Congress-led government of Ibobi Singh completed the full tenure, which was a milestone in the political history of Manipur since 1967. The electorate seemed to have taken a stand in favour of stability, which none but the Congress could ensure.[7] Second, the Meitei's emotional position in favour of united Manipur, led the majority of this ethnic segment of the state to support the national party, which, in all probability, would protect the territorial integrity of the state, despite the fact that the Congress-led UPA government at the Centre was committed to continue the peace dialogue with the NSCN (IM). The BJP's intention in this regard was doubted by most of the Meiteis, because the NDA government's announcement of some concession to the Nagalim demand was an indication that peace in Nagaland could be purchased at the cost of united Manipur. Third, there could be post-poll arrangement between the Congress and the NSCN (IM), should the former fail to secure absolute majority in the legislature with the latter reaping electoral harvest of its expectation. The conglomeration of the regional forces and the BJP would be too weak and self-serving to show any sign of dislodging the Congress. Fourth, the MPP as a new platform for unity of thought and action representing regionalism, failed to enlist the required popular trust and confidence, because of the presence of a host of leaders like Rajkumar Dorendra Singh who had changed his political affiliation more than thrice.

It is important to note that the first phase of the elections slated for February 8, 2007 covered 19 constituencies out of which 6 constituencies, viz, 43,44,45, 47, 48, and 49, are Naga dominated, with constituency numbers 50 and 51 being Kuki dominated, while the rest are mostly Meitei inhabited. These are the constituencies where insurgency was active, and hence, were considered to be very sensitive ones. These were expected to the forerunners of the election trend, in respect of voters' turnout, if the elections could be conducted peacefully with encouraging turnout, the second phase scheduled for February 14, covering 29 constituencies known to be Meitei dominated, would presumably follow this trend. With the remaining 12 constituencies, out of which 6 are Kuki dominated, free from any trouble on the election-day. There was an almost incontrovertible logic behind such an assessment: the UNC would give a call to the Nagas to cast their votes *en bloc* and *en masse* in favour of its candidates, so that all the 11 UNC contestants would score emphatic victory and eventually would have a significantly position to raise a solid voice in the Assembly for Naga integration i.e. for Nagalim. High turnout in the Naga areas would induce the Meiteis to respond in a befitting manner, and there would be heavy turnout in the constituencies in the second phase. Heavy turnout would be a referendum on a number of issues.

Despite militancy there was enthusiasm among the political parties and the electorate regarding the elections. The enthusiasm was well channelized by the Congress, which had already demonstrated its preparedness for the elections much before the announcement of the poll. The need to ensure stability, for the continuation of the development agenda for another five years, had already been conveyed to the people by the well-tailored speeches of the Chief Minister in public meetings. In every speech, Chief Minister Ibobi Singh attributed his success to the party. "Congress means stability and continuity, so vote for Congress, which in any case will form the next government", he exhorted.[8] This was in addition to the achievements on the economic front, law and order situation, employment generation and eradication of poverty, education and health needs etc. These exercises were tried to offset the incumbency factor playing a negative role against the Congress and the Chief Minister.

The moods of the political parties and the general public were up beat but divergent with a variety of reason and expectations. The ruling party geared up its poll machinery fully and accelerated the process of mobilization of its support base for an emphatic victory. The MPP and other regional parties took the opportunity to campaign for the withdrawal of the AFSPA. The NSCN (IM) supporting the UNC drew up its strategy to capture all the seven seats in the Naga dominated areas, and thereby, wanted to spearhead its movement for Naga unity in a wider context, through parliamentary procedure. The announcement of the elections offered a plank for other ethnic based parties and groups to raise their voice. It rightly seemed that, for diverse reasons, the 2007 elections were going to be exiting.

Once the UNC decided to field its own candidates and targeted to capture at least 11 seats in the 60-member Assembly, the scope of pre and post poll violence was dramatically reduced. It may be by accident or by design that the first phase of elections scheduled for February 8, 2007 covered the constituencies known to be strongholds of the Naga communities, whose positive response to electioneering and turnout on the day of the poll would definitely contribute to the smooth conduct of elections in all the constituencies.

REFERENCES

1. http://en.wikipedia.org/wiki/Elections
2. For some noteworthy studies on the success of coalition politics in India see Mahendra Prasad Singh and Anil Misra (eds), *Coalition Politics in India and Prospects* (New Delhi: Manohar, 2004) and Bidyut Chakrabarty, *Forging Power: Coalition Politics in India* (New Delhi: Oxford University Press, 2006) and Paul R. Brass, "Coalition Politics in North India", *American Political Science Review*, Vol. 62, No. 4, December 1968, pp. 1174-1191.
3. Elizabeth Devi Kh., "Political Instability in Manipur: Nature and Causes", an unpublished working paper (Guwahati: OKDISCD, 2003).
4. Political defection had already started with the split of the Congress at the national level after the 1967 Lok Sabha elections. Its impact was felt in a number of states. For some details see Subhash C. Kashyap, *The Politics of Defection: A Study of State Politics in India* (New Delhi: Continental Publishing House, 1969).
5. For details see *Sangai Express*, December 30, 2006.
6. For details see *The Sentinel*, February 5, 2007.
7. Based on our discussion with scholars, journalist and a candidates belonging to the both ruling and the Opposition parties.
8. Sekhar Dutta, "CM sees life beyond five", *The Telegraph*, February 3, 2007.

4

ALLIANCES FORMATION AND ISSUES

In the Indian political setting, two types of alliance have been experimented at the national as well as at the state levels – pre and post-election alliance. The historic pre-poll alliance among the four non-Congress national parties that had taken place just before the Lok Sabha elections in 1977 was a watershed in the election politics in India. At the state level, the West Bengal and the Kerala model had set an example for others. The post-poll alliance as in 1996 which led to the formation of National Democratic Alliance, and then in 2004 leading to the emergence of the United Progressive Alliance are examples of workable political adjustment in an era of coalition politics in India.

Manipur has had the experience of the both pre- and post-poll alliance for four decades. The Secular Progressive Front (SPF), formed by the Indian National Congress (INC) and the Communist Party of India (CPI) in 2002 to form the government headed by Okram Ibobi Singh, was the forerunner of alliance building in the state. It is noteworthy that alliance making eventually led to merger of parties. A few instances are presented here to understand the peculiarities of the state politics in Manipur.

Manipur People's Party

Pre-poll alliance may have been totally unheard of in the state politics of Manipur. Such an idea was foreign to the state till the 9th Manipur Legislative Assembly Election. Just before the elections held in 2007, two regional forces, the Federal Party of Manipur (FPM) and the Democratic Revolutionary People's Party (DRPP), set an example of pre-poll alliance formation. The FPM and the DRPP agreed upon to merge with the MPP, the oldest regional party in the state which came up with a regional agenda in 1972. The MPP emerged as the umbrella organization of all the former regional parties in the state. It presented an encouraging prospect of enlisting the support of electorate having a pro-regional sentiment and offering a formidable challenge to the ruling Congress party.

Reasons for alliance or merger under the banner of MPP were clear and understandable. The regional forces believed that a resurgent Manipur was possible under a regional forum, having a deep commitment to preserve the territorial integrity of the state and to its culture, tradition, language and history; it would eventually make Manipur a vibrant state. Such a commitment would usher in a predictable revitalization of its economy and restore socio-political order, which have been a far cry for the last four decades. More importantly, they felt a joint endeavour would dislodge the Congress-led political arrangement from power.

This umbrella organization tried but failed to bring into its fold another regional formation, created by the

Manipur Democratic Peoples Party (MDPP), which decided to merge with the Manipur State Congress Party (MSCP). The MDPP is a regional party which was formed by some breakaway members of the state BJP, a few months ahead of the election. This group snapped all its relations with the BJP, as it had grave differences on regional issues and problems, including the territorial integrity of Manipur, activities at the grassroots levels where development matters overshadow the Hindutva agenda, and more importantly on the demand for the withdrawal of the AFSPA, 1958. There were patent reasons behind the merger of the MDPP with the MSCP, such as to gear up efforts for economic development in the state and to uphold the territorial integrity of Manipur.[1]

United Naga Democratic Front

A new front emerged just before the elections, reportedly with the blessings of the NSCN (IM); it was a front made by the consensus Independent candidates selected and sponsored by the United Naga Council (UNC). Christened as 'United Naga Democratic Front' (UNDF) with S. Kho John as its convenor, who was to operate in consultation with the UNC, the Front stood up as the representative of the Naga people living in the state of Manipur. It decided to have a common flag and common election symbol. The colour of the flag was to be blue while its symbol, a candle. The statement signed by nine consensus independent candidates of United Naga Council said that the alliance would operate as pre-poll and post-poll alliance in order to fulfill the aims of the 'common manifesto', as announced in the UNC's position paper, which clearly stated that integration of all Naga inhabited areas under one political framework was the principal objective of the Council. The nine signatories, as UNC's consensus Independent candidates were - Samuel Jendai of the Tamenglong, Danny Shaiza of Ukhrul, Wungnaoshang Keishing of Phungyar, Dr. Khasim Ruivah of Chingai, Awangbow Newmei of Tamei, RV Shirang of Karong, K. Raina of Tadubi, S.Kho John of Mao and Morung Makunga of Tengnoupal Assembly constituencies. The UNDF further added that the alliance would function in and outside the Assembly after being elected to achieve the objective of the manifesto, important points of which include that the alliance will mobilize the people for fullest support to the ongoing Indo-Naga political dialogue for an honourable solution and to provide leadership to the society in nation building.[2]

The Samajwadi Party tried to forge an alliance with some other non-Congress Parties such as the CPI and the RJD, but failed to proceed ahead to a logical and desired end. To put it precisely, there were two alliance formations – the regional parties under the banner of the MPP and the MSCP, leading to merger of constituents under broad frameworks. The UNDF could not be treated as an alliance, for, it was the common election platform of the UNC backed by the NSCN (IM).

The issues

Too many issues obfuscated the electorate in the Assembly 2007 elections, although it is quite natural that every political party tends to bring out a list of issues for public consumption and for an action-oriented agenda to be pursued, if its candidates are returned to the Assembly. The commitment to the issues could be treated as election promises to be redeemed during the tenure, if elected. They are expressed through the medium of manifestos of the respective parties. Some of the issues figured in the election manifestos of the political parties in the state may be briefly stated for understanding of the political environment under which the 2007 elections were held.

The question of ***Territorial Integrity*** of Manipur came out as one of the most important issues, which found prominence in each and every manifesto. Every party, with the exception of the UNC and the UNDF, made it as the most important poll issue in the 9th Assembly election in the backdrop of the Nagas claim for 'Nagalim' and pledged to protect and uphold the territorial integrity of the State. The national and the regional political parties – be it the Congress, the BJP, the RJD, the NCP, the LJP, the CPI, the CPI(M), the SP, the MSCP, the MPP or, the Janata Dal (Secular) – all made it unequivocally clear that the integrity of the state of Manipur was their prime concern and that it would be defended at all possible cost. They all maintained that the survival of the people of Manipur, and hence, the survival of the political parties depend entirely upon the survival of the state, without erosion of a single inch of land. All the parties published their manifestos in the Meitei and other local languages so as to reach the common masses. The manifestos were widely distributed among the electorate, right from the 'flag hoisting day' observed by each and every political party.

The Congress Party, in the introductory remarks of its manifesto, made it clear that its primary objective was to protect and defend the territorial integrity of the state, none should doubt this commitment.

Likewise, the Rashtriya Janta Dal (RJD), in its manifesto, stated that Manipur has been in existence, having its own boundary and people of different ethnic groups in different faiths speaking different languages, for more than 2000 years. Therefore, any threat to the territorial integrity and unity of the state would be strongly confronted. Effective measures such as cultivating the 'Unity of Minds' among the people were sought to be accelerated to meet any possible challenges coming from any corner. The Left parties, such as the CPI (M) promised to fight communal ideology on the issue of territorial boundary whereas the CPI pledged for the protection of the unique features of the state in the line with Jananeta Irabat's struggle for unity among peoples. The Manipur Peoples Party, a strong platform of regional forces, stated in its election manifesto that the issue of territorial integrity of Manipur, a land of different ethnic groups, was at the top of its political agenda and called for preserving unity and territorial integrity.

The Manipur State Congress Party (MSCP) cited historical records to prove that Manipur was an ancient sovereign kingdom with clearly defined and demarcated territorial boundaries, even when it was annexed to the British Empire in 1891. The territorial demarcation remained unaffected throughout the recent period of history including the day of India's independence, the merger agreement of 15th October 1949 and the adoption of the Indian Union and Boundary of Manipur provision of Section 3 of the North Eastern Areas (Reorganization) Act, 1971. Therefore, the party pledged to protect and preserve the territorial and emotional integrity of the people of Manipur.

The Armed Forces (Special Powers) Act, 1958, has been a hot issue in the state for a considerably long period of time. There has been a series of agitations and movements, including naked demonstration[3] in front of the Kangla fort on July 15, 2004 to register the demand for the withdrawal of the 'black and draconian law'. As such, it was not unusual to find demand for its withdrawal in the manifestos of all the political parties. It appears that no political party could go to the electorate without expressing strong views against the Act; that is why it became a hot poll issue and found a place in the manifesto of every political party. The Congress claimed that the Secular Progressive Front (SPF) coalition government led by Okram Ibobi Singh had withdrawn AFSPA from 7 Assembly segments in Imphal Municipal area, in public interest. The party, if voted to power, promised to improve the law and order situation, so that, the Act could be completely withdrawn from all parts of the state. During her first campaign visit to the state, the UPA Chief, Sonia Gandhi, assured the electorate that the AFSPA would be withdrawn phase-wise. Other parties such as the BJP, the SP, the RJD, the MPP and the MSCP promised to take necessary steps to withdraw the Act. All these parties considered that the enforcement of the controversial Act was a cruel step infringing on the basic human rights. There was no different opinion on this matter. It was apparently a very strong election issue for all the political parties.

The Leftist CPI, which was a party to the coalition SPF Government, took the credit for getting the AFSPA withdrawn from 7 Assembly constituencies in Imphal Municipal Area. Further, the party claimed that it had been working hard to get the Act withdrawn from the rest of the state. It argued that in conformity with the recommendation of the Justice B.P. Jeevan Reddy Commission and in order to save the life of Irom

Sharmila, who has been on hunger strike since November 4, 2000[4], soon after the Malom incident in which several civilians lost their life as a result of firing by Assam Rifles personnel. The CPI (M) also made it an election issue and pledged to continue its efforts on the same lines in order to ensure the security of innocent civilian life and to protect individuals against the misuse of the draconian law. It promised to take steps to spearhead democratic movements to get the Act withdrawn from the state.

The MPP, in its election manifesto (under the heading, Governance and political system) considered the Act an important poll issue and placed it at the top of its agenda for action stating that this controversial Act, despite being in force in the State for the past 30 years, had not yet yielded the desired result, but created chaos and wrought havoc. The Act, instead of bringing down insurgency, had led to its increase. It further emphatically declared that the Act had caused gross violation of human rights. It appreciated the recommendations made by the Jeevan Reddy Commission and argued that such an Act must not operate in the state[5]. Therefore, it pledged to work for the withdrawal of the Act as soon as possible in order ensure protection of civil and human rights of the common citizen.

The Manipur State Congress Party, another regional party, made an identical pledge to work for the end of the enforcement of the AFSPA, 1958.

The UNC as well as the UNDF distanced itself from the issue of the withdrawal of the AFSPA. It appeared that their agenda was to capture all the eleven constituencies where the Nagas have a demographic advantage by raising the issue of integration of the Naga inhabited areas. Other issues, in this process, got sidelined.

Insurgency is a hot issue for the entire state of Manipur. The state has been suffering grievously for more than three decades as a result of insurgency related violence and counter insurgency operations. As stated in Chapter I, the state has been bleeding with the blood of countless people. Although all the peace loving people of the state wanted peace consequent on conflict transformation, peace remains illusive till the date.[6] The Manipur People's Party, a conglomeration of three regional parties, has been vocal ever since its formation in support of making serious efforts to bring about a political solution to the insurgency problem through dialogue across the negotiation table, while the MSCP, another regional forum maintained a discreet silence on the issue of insurgency in its manifesto.

The national parties like Rashtriya Janta Dal (RJD) took a lead in pledging that revolutionary movements in Manipur needed to be handled through a composite political dialogue between the Government of India and the rebel groups. They suggested that efforts could be initiated at the national and international levels so that peace returned to the state without any further delay. There is no difference of opinion on the need to find a solution to the current insurgency problem through dialogue, and therefore, all the political parties - both national and regional - had a consensus of opinion in proposing an all-out endeavour to bring the rebel groups to the negotiation table. The Congress manifesto put emphasis not only on resolution of the insurgency through a composite dialogue but also advocated rehabilitation of the youth who had already returned to the mainstream.

The issue of better ***surface connectivity*** figured prominently in all the manifestos of the various political parties, for, Manipur is known to be one of most ill-connected states in the country. The road transport is in bad shape and connectivity to remote and hill areas is minimal and deplorable. So is the condition of important roads, such as, Imphal to Moreh and Imphal to Nagaland border. Naturally, the issue of better surface connectivity became an important poll plank for all the political parties.

The partners of the Secular Progressive Front headed by Okram Ibobi Singh – the Congress and the CPI - put emphasis on the task of economic and infrastructure development in the state. The issue of connectivity through road transport figured prominently in the in their respective manifestos, for, it was argued that road connectivity was the key to economic development. On the transportation front Congress promised that work for Silchar-Jiribam Tupul–Imphal rail line which was taken as a national project would be completed soon. It claimed that the work of the 4-lane National Highway-39 had already started at its initiative during the tenure of Okram Ibobi Singh. It pledged that the East West Express Highway from Saurastra to Silchar would be further extended by 105 km up to Moreh via Imphal, as a part of the Asian Highway. The old Cachar road popularly known as Tongjei Maril, would be converted to NH-53 and the Thinungei–Jiribam Road to NH-150. The construction and improvement of Guite Road would be taken up soon under the North Eastern Council (NEC) programme. The inter-district and inter-village roads would be developed for better connectivity. The Congress highlighted the need to have better railways for easy and economic transportation which would ensure steady economic development of the state. Therefore, it promised to complete all the pending railway and highway projects, if voted back to power. It also pledged to improve the water transport system, which has been functioning in certain places in Manipur, connecting the hills with the plain areas.

Echoing the same slogan, 'development through surface connectivity', the CPI promised to create an effective task force named as the Highway Protection Force to ensure safety and security of traffic and of passengers in view of frequent occurrence of incidents of extortion by the underground outfits on highways and other declared and undeclared bandhs. Such a force would be expected to deal with the problem of disruption of communications, for days and weeks together, owing to agitational programmes, such as, road blockade calls given by different civil society organizations.

The RJD, in its manifesto, promised to construct and improve all the connecting roads linking remote areas to all the District headquarters by a circular highway, increase the frequency of bus services and to install rope ways, rope trucks, rope cars to ensure greater connectivity in the hill areas. It also promised to speed up the construction work of the railway line from Jiribam to Tupul onto Imphal at the positive intervention of the Union Railway Minister Lalu Prasad Yadav, who happened to the President of the RJD.

The BJP promises paid more attention to the construction of inter village roads in order to improve the conditions of the rural people.

The MSCP pledged to constitute a "State Mission on Communication Infrastructure Building" which would work for bringing a solution to the existing and perennial problems long associated with (i) civil road transport connectivity (ii) tele-communication and (ii) delay in the construction of railways.

The SP, the CPI and the CPI(M), in their respective manifestos, included the issue of promoting better surface connectivity through roads, railways and waterways. All of them paid importance to the current plan of action of converting the existing road from Imphal to Moreh to a four-lane highway, in order to promote international trade. All of them emphasized the need to have effective highway and railway protection forces for safety and security of the passengers and vehicular traffic.

To put it precisely, surface connectivity has been a major agenda inseparably connected with the economic development of the state. It is interesting to find that such an important issue did not figure in the manifestos of the MPP and the NCP. They paid more importance to other volatile issues such as the problem of insurgency, the repeal of AFSPA, the failure of the Ibobi Government and so on.

Power shortage is one of the most important issues highlighted in the agenda of almost all political parties of the state. Manipur has been a power deficit state as stated in Chapter II (Table 2.8). The abundance of natural resources, such as rivers and the Loktak lake, could not play the role of a natural boon to steer the state from power deficit to a power-surplus one. The weak power regime is a discouraging factor in planning for industrialization of the state. Therefore, almost all the political parties made it an election issue and pledged for their commitment to power generation. The

Oktam Ibobi Singh government had already taken steps to harness electricity under the Loktak Down Stream Project and it promised to accelerate the process of completing the same on time. It also pledged to improve the power situaticn by undertaking the micro hydel projects at suitable places, like Tuivai and Irang, and to increase the quantum of power generated by Leimakhong Heavy Fuel Power Project. The party promised to electrify all the villages of Manipur by 2009. There were other promises too, such as, of ceaseless efforts to electrify all households under the Rajiv Gandhi Grameen Vidyutikaran Yojna (RGVY).

Other parties too did not lag behind in making commitments to generate power so that the current power deficit could be properly addressed and to make the state a power-surplus one. The RJD believed that power supply in the state was very low, so much so that one could not run even a small industry smoothly. With the present power supply unable to meet daily necessities, the party promised to prepare a unique plan for generating sufficient power. Other National Parties like the BJP and the SP did not talk much on power. While the BJP in its manifesto pledged to launch the Tipaimukh Dam Project as soon as possible, the SP advocated small hydel power projects and the alternative methodology of bio-diesel power production to tide over the current energy crisis. The MPP supported the environmentalists in opposing the construction of Tipaimukh hydel dam, apprehending ecological imbalance and pleaded for small dams for power generation. The MSCP virtually ignored the issue, and did not mention anything in its manifesto. The CPI made a passing reference to the issue while making a commitment to constitute an expert committee to look into the pros and cons of the Tipaimukh Dam, and made a commitment to provide electricity to every household at an affordable rate.

Rejuvenating the rural economy of Manipur was one of the major election planks for most of the political parties in the 2007 Assembly elections. Manipur is a rural state where 76 per cent of the people lives in rural areas. The economy is basically rural and therefore, agriculture is the mainstay of 99.5 per cent rural population. Naturally, all the political parties could not but highlight the problems and prospects of rejuvenating the rural economy in order to attract the rural electorate. Therefore, a number of agriculture related matters figured nearly all the manifestos.

Almost all the parties accorded a lot of importance to a number of issues associated with agriculture sector, viz, development of agricultural infrastructure including farm mechanization and use of fertilizer, investment in crop diversification and multiple cropping, introduction of high yielding varieties and better irrigation. The Congress party took the lead in framing an integrated strategy for the rejuvenation of this primary sector. The strategy included, among others as stated above, protection of cultivable land, provision of soft loan to farmers, encouragement of organic farming of horticultural produce, crop insurance schemes and fixation of support prices, and promotion of floriculture, horticulture and pisiculture. Highlighting the achievement of the government in its uninterrupted tenure of five years, the Congress party took the credit for expansion of irrigation projects, under Bharat Nirman and other multi-purpose projects already underway in Khuga, Thoubal and Doliathabi. It promised to have more activities under the Horticulture Technology Mission to boost horticulture farming in the hill areas of Manipur. It also promised to extend help to the mulberry farmers and to promote the sericulture sector.

The CPI, being a partner in the Secular Progressive Front government, had almost a similar manifesto, containing promises to accelerate the development of agricultural economy and to expand the avenues for rural livelihood. It pleaded for formulation of a sound agricultural policy for the state.

Other national parties like the BJP and the SP did not prepare elaborate manifestos, to make revitalization of the rural economy and livelihood a prominent agenda for development of Manipur. The NCP promised to spearhead a green revolution by making massive state investment in the agriculture sector. It paid adequate attention to proper and extensive irrigation, introduction of multiple cropping and high yielding crops to achieve the objective of transforming Manipur into a vibrant agriculture-rich state.

The RJD made a general statement of special attention to introduce advanced technology for agriculture in the plains and for horticulture in the hill areas and a policy for protection of agriculture and cultivable land.

The MPP promised to facilitate extensive use of scientific methods to increase agricultural produce in the state. It put strong emphasis on the plantation of fruit-yielding plants and on food processing industry, so as to create more opportunities for self-employment. The other regional party, the MSCP, in its manifesto promised to undertake massive training programmes for the youths, farmers and women in the field of food preservation, processing, packaging and marketing. To augment agricultural facilities, the MSCP promised to take up river lift irrigation, tapping soft ground water and harvesting of rain water for extensive cultivation and double/triple cropping in the state.

It is interesting to note that the national parties like the BJP and the SP left out these issues, and did not make these part of their election planks.

Industries, Trade and Commerce did not find much space in the election manifestos of most of the parties. It is mainly because of the fact that Manipur is an industrially backward state with hardly any bright prospect of dramatic change in the scenario, for reasons of bad connectivity, insurgency and paucity of resources both human and natural. Trade and commerce had been adversely affected by political instability, insurgency and extortion; some of the political parties tried to put these issues before the electorate. The CPI is one of such parties, which pledged to fully exploit all natural and human resources, for a self-reliant economy in which industry and trade and commerce would have their due natural stake. It promised to establish agro-based, sericulture-based and forest based industries, besides cultivating opportunities for developing tourism into a viable industry. Further, it gave the commitment to revigorate the already vibrant small scale and cottage industries to the fullest extent, besides, of course, expanding the facilities for marketing locally and exporting the handloom and handicraft products.

The issue of trade and commerce figured in the manifestos of almost all the political parties with different degrees of importance paid to these. The question of expansion of trade and commerce, for enhancing the prospects of livelihood and widening the Indo-Myanmar trade which had the potentiality of creating better job and livelihood opportunities in the informal sectors, captured the attention of the political parties contesting the 2007 elections.

The Congress, being the front-runner in the election campaign and heading the incumbent government, echoed the same slogan of promoting bilateral trade between India and Myanmar and of bringing the South East Asian Countries into the trade fold of the region in which the state of Manipur would play the role of a gateway. It also promised employment generation for youth through the promotion of handloom, handicraft and food processing sectors.

Other political parties such as the NCP and the SP pledged to give attention to the thrust areas of agro-based and forest based industries, khadi, handicraft and other small scale industries in order to improve the conditions in the rural areas, and to creation of infrastructure for the production and marketing of small volume and high value items such as electronic goods.

The MPP too covered these issues in its manifesto. It believed that promotion and pro-active steps on similar lines would rejuvenate the rural economy of Manipur.

Interestingly enough, the national parties, the BJP and the RJD, and a regional party, the MSCP, remained silent on these issues, vital to the economy of the state. Furthermore, these are considered to be catchy issues which deservedly draw the attention of the rural electorate constituting the bulk of the population.

Look East Policy is one of the issues that had been highlighted by almost all political parties in their manifestos. Manipur, bordering Myanmar, could be treated as the first entry point of India's North East to the countries in South East Asia. The inflow and outflow of trade and commerce between this region and the rest of South East Asia, begins at Moreh; therefore, Manipur stands on a strategically important locus of international trade and commerce. The recent discourse on 'Look East Policy' involves Manipur along with the other states of the region. Consequently, this state is expected to play a crucial role in the entire effort towards operationalization of the said policy.

Being aware of the recent developments in the matter of pursuing the 'Look East Policy' to usher new vistas for mutually beneficial relations and opportunities, almost all the political parties affirmed their support for the policy with the high expectation that it would bring fortune to the state. It has been found that the regional forums like the MPP and the MSCP adopted a positive attitude towards the said policy; and they believed that a Special Economic Zone (SEZ) at Moreh could be established to boost the economic activities centering around international trade and commerce and also tourism. Other political parties such as the Congress, the NCP, the CPI and the CPI(M) were unanimous in their stand to take full advantage of 'Look East Policy'. To them the promotion of international trade and commerce with Myanmar and other East Asian countries was key to the successful operation of the policy. Considering the geographical location of the state and its status of a vast repository of natural and human resources, they pledged to work for capacity building of the people of Manipur to enable them to face the challenges posed by the new initiatives under the said policy. They promised to take necessary steps to expand the market of Manipur's traditional commodities in East Asian and the ASEAN countries. Along with these, they promised to draw a viable plan to exchange culture and literature, in order to strengthen the already existing traditional ties with these neighbours. They felt that exchange of youth-related programmes would enhance better relationship among the people living in this vast geographical area.

It is striking that the BJP, the RJD and the SP had the least to talk on the policy, and virtually remained silent on it.

Education was another important poll issue for almost all the parties as put forward through their respective election manifestos. The insurgency situation, coupled with economic backwardness, had affected adversely the education scenario in the state. The media had been focusing on the problem of outflow of students from Mainpur for better education elsewhere. Therefore, almost all the political parties promised to work for a better academic environment in the state. The Congress promised to create better opportunities for quality education. Its manifesto took the pride for having done magnificent work in this field and claimed the credit of converting the Manipur University into a Central one. The manifesto contained the loud promises to provide free and compulsory education up to class XII for students belonging to the SC/ST, the minorities and the OBC groups under Below Poverty Level (BPL). The party also pledged to offer computer education courses from class III, and to step up various career guidance programmes for the students in the state.

The CPI, as a coalition partner of the SPF government, made commitment on the similar lines and talked of modernization of the education system. It advocated allocation of 30% of the state budget on education in order to achieve total literacy in the state and to provide for free and compulsory education to all children up to the age of eighteen years. It put strong emphasis on efforts to make full use of Sarva Shiksha Abhiyan Scheme. In addition, it made a commitment to initiate changes in the education system and to reorient the school syllabi in order that students imbibe the spirit of tolerance, brotherhood, secularism and national integration. It argued in favour of formulation of a special policy to improve the aided and private educational institutions.

The NCP emphasized the need for earmarking 6 per cent of the GDP investment for the development of education. It further emphasized universalization of elementary education and also demanded for an IIT (Indian Institute of Technology) and an IIM (Indian Institute of Management) in the State.

The RJD took up the issue of development of human resource as an important agenda. To ensure qualitative improvement in the overall scenario in the state it promised to frame a policy of transfer and posting of teachers of schools and colleges and to entrust recruitment of teachers to an independent/autonomous body to ensure fair, impartial and transparent selection.

The CPI (M) in its manifesto showed concern at the deplorable condition of the government and government-aided schools on the one hand and the mushroom growth of private schools/institutes on the other. It held that such a situation had laid devastating impact on child's education, detrimental to overall growth in the state. It promised to provide free and compulsory education up to the secondary level, and also pleaded for 30% budget allocation for education 6% GDP allocation for one IIT and one IIM. The CPI(M) position on education resembled that of the CPI and the NCP. There was only one new agenda in the CPI(M) manifesto. It promised to open, at least one, library in every town of Manipur.

The MPP and the MSCP also promised to increase the budget allocation on education to 6% from the present 2% and pledged for common text books both for hill areas and the plains. They were in favour of formulation of a state education policy and introduction of technical and skill development courses at the 10-12th standard. The SP joined the two regional parties in advocating for the introduction of such courses at high and higher secondary levels.

The BJP did not elaborate its plan of action for the improvement in the educational scenario in the state.

Health, like education, received importance in the manifestos of all the national and regional parties contesting the 2007 elections. Within the larger frame of the subject of health, the lead issue, which drew the attention of one and all, was the problem of HIV/AIDS, for the obvious reason that Manipur is one the worst affected states. It is reported that Manipur has a severe problem of HIV positive affected people, which accounts for 14.44% of all India cases.[7] Young people below the age of 30 years constitute the major percentage of such cases (73.52). Close on the heels of this almost unmitigated problem, a study reveals that a high prevalence of HIV infection among injecting drug users in Manipur increased at an alarming rate.[8] It is reported that there are about 2,866 cases of HIV/AIDS infected patients[9], and the two Imphal districts have dubious record of high percentage (Table 4.1) of such cases. Naturally, it has been a grave health problem, which concern all the conscious citizens of the state.

Table 4.1
District-wise HIV/AIDS cases in percentage

Sl.No.	*Districts*	%
1	Imphal East & West	68.83
2	Thoubal	9.06
3	Churachandpur	6.02
4	Bishnupur	4.91
5	Chandel	3.66
6	Senapati	3.65
7	Ukhrul	3.60
8	Tamenglong	0.26

Source: Rajen Irengbam, "HIV/AIDS Epidemic in Manipur" www.manipuronline.com

The Congress put the problem at the top of health concerns covered by its manifesto. All other parties, too, paid similar attention and expressed concern at the growing statistics of HIV/AIDS afflicted patients. It promised to allocate separate fund in the State budget for HIV/AIDS, to carry on vigorously the prevention programmes. It wanted to use the Local Area Development fund of MLAs to promote the AIDS awareness programmes, in their respective constituencies. It pledged to press into service the government health department to spearhead a movement to control this grave health hazard.

HIV/AIDS has been a poll issue with the NCP, the RJD, the CPI (M), the MPP and the MSCP. All these party pledged to adopt intensive measures and use State government's financial allocation for combating the disease. Parties like the CPI, the BJP and the SP, however, left out the issue in their poll manifestos.

Almost all the contesting parties took up this issue as a major election plank. There was no difference of opinion as to the approach to sensitize the public about this ailment and the ways and means to control it. Since the preventive measures and awareness programmes are cost-driven exercises, most of the political parties talked of augmenting central resources, including the one called "Non-Lapsable Central Pool of Resources" (NLCPR).

Some of the parties brought out specific issues. The NCP pledged to re-activate rural health care centers and to upgrade the J. N. Hospital, the only State hospital with better amenities. Two contesting leftist parties, the CPI and the CPI(M), pleaded for substantial increase in the investment on public health and on extension to all villages of primary health centers to be equipped with competent staff, infrastructure and adequate stock of medicine.

Women & Child Development was another important issue which received attention of all the political parties. The two left parties were eloquent in making clear commitment to ensure gender equality and women empowerment in all fields through integrated plans for housewives so that they could participate effectively in the process of decision–making within and outside the household. They pleaded for reservation of seats in all elective and democratic bodies. The RJD, in its manifesto, strongly decried the exploitation of women in social or political life and pledged for the upliftment of women's status. It promised to prepare a framework for reducing gender discrimination and for bringing women to play a positive role in the development process in the state. These parties considered women and children as the most vulnerable segment in the social milieu that needed adequate protection against exploitation. Like them, the NCP, while preparing an identical manifesto for women and children advocated special policy planning for the welfare of these two weaker sections of the society.

The two regional parties, the MPP and the MSCP, took up the issue of reservation for women in all elective bodies and in filling certain percentage of posts in order to ensure gender justice and promote equality. They favoured an integrated plan for the promotion of women entrepreneurship, so that they could play a role in small and large business ventures. They promised to offer soft loan to women through State Apex Cooperative Banks, so that they could start business independently. Through such measures, they hoped to bring women to the centre stage of economic development of the state.

The Congress Party claimed in its manifesto to have done much for women's empowerment. It took the credit for setting up the State Women Commission with the objective of looking after the problems of women and promoting their welfare. Now it promised to set up a separate court to deal with cases relating to women so that speedy and fair trial of women-related litigations could be ensured. It also proposed to strengthen women police force to reduce the possibility of violence against women at the hands of male police. It also promised to extend financial assistance and loans to deserving women, seeking self employment, and Women Self Help Groups, as also to create more government jobs for women, promote women's education and initiate measures towards universal immunization of children against diseases. It made commitment to improve the health care and nutrition services for children and to institutionalize mid-day meal schemes throughout the state, so that school going children were better looked after and school dropout rate could be brought down.

The issues of ***minority, other backward classes Scheduled Castes / Scheduled Tribes*** figured in the election manifestos of most of the parties. No political party in India can afford to ignore these at the election time, because of their volatility and sensitive nature. The INC claimed to have redeemed some of its promises made in the previous election manifesto, by setting up a Minority Commission and an OBC Commission. This time it promised to take up various programmes for the removal of grievances of these groups of people for all-round development. It also pledged to construct more hostels for SC/ST girls and boys and for Muslim girls and to augment resources to advance financial assistance for medical treatment of needy patients, belonging to the minority communities and the OBC.

Other political parties such as the NCP and the MPP made general statements on the need to uplift the conditions of these socio-religious groups and did not speak of any special programme or agenda.

The MSCP, however, mentioned about the need to formulate a welfare policy for the Scheduled Castes and development of an institutional mechanism to improve their lot. It is interesting to note that the party left out the minorities, the Scheduled Tribes and for the OBC from its promotional agenda. Likewise the BJP and the RJD remained silent on these issues.

Art and Culture featured in the manifestos of all the political parties. It is quite natural in view of the fact that Manipur is acknowledged as one of the most vibrant states in matters of art and culture. All the political parties spoke about their commitment to preservation and promotion of the rich cultural heritage of the state, as also development of all forms of art, theatre, music and dance forms. Most of the parties emphasized the need to expedite the renovation of the Kangla fort, and of securing the status of a world heritage site for it. Most of the political parties gave importance to the renovation of the all historical sites, monuments and buildings which bear the imprints of the past history of the state. The Congress and other regional parties expressed their commitment to set up a national school for art and music in Manipur.

The CPI pledged to transform the historic Kangla Fort into a grand and glamorous ecological park, which would also be treated as a historical site and a place of tourist attraction. It joined the chorus for the promotion and preservation of all historically important places and for the development of traditional martial arts. It pledged to give due recognition to all writers, musicians, theatre personalities and performers of traditional martial arts. Interestingly enough, the MPP, which is a strong regional party, did not come forward with a specific programme on these issues

The NCP pledged to formulate a cultural policy to preserve the rich culture of the State, while the BJP gave its commitment to open new avenues for the proper training, infrastructural facilities and exposure to young sports and cultural talents by taking them outside the state and the country. It promised to create separate funds for such activities.

Games and Sports figured as an election issue in almost all the manifestos. Manipur in this context, one of the most forward states in the country, usually steals the show in national games. For the last couple of years it has been at the top of medals tally in the national games, and its sports personalities have earned laurels in international events. Therefore, most of the parties promised to work out proper youth and sports policy to encourage the ever-growing numbers of leading sportspersons of the state. Some of the parties like the NCP and the MPP talked of development and promotion of indigenous games and sports for their uniqueness. The Congress brought out a scheme for the development of sports infrastructure at schools, villages and panchayat areas throughout the state under Panchayat Yuva Shakti Khel Aviyan and construction of mini stadium so as to enable the youth to take part in sports locally.

Other relevant issues

A number of other issues figured in the manifestos of various political parties with varied degree of importance attached. A couple of these are, the need to promote science and technology and information technology, for development of IT connectivity throughout the state. The issue of environment protection also came up in the manifestos of almost all the political parties. It figured in the context of use and protection of rivers, lakes and water bodies and also arguments for and against the construction of Tipaimukh dam. Some other issues, such as devolution of administrative and financial power on the panchayati raj institutions, in the light of the 73rd amendment and improvement of the municipal self-governance within the framework of 74th amendment received attention of most of the political parties. While the Congress took the credit for implementing the objectives of the two landmark constitutional amendments, the opposition parties leveled strong criticism of its failure in devolving power on the elected bodies in letter and spirit. It is interesting to note that the administration and functioning of the Sixth Scheduled areas[10] did not get due attention from most of political parties. Only a few of them made some passing reference to it, despite the fact that there had been occasional allegations that the all the six District Councils were unable to redeem the objectives for which they were created, either because of corruption or because of the lack of interest on the part of the state government in extending the desired support.

The positions taken by various political parties on the issue of promotion of tourism in the state, appeared to be confusing and contradictory. While most of the political parties pledged to promote tourism to the extent of transforming it into a viable industry, some of them, more particularly, the regional parties, were arguing in favour of retaining the Restricted Area Permit and Inner Line Permission, which are known to be formidable discouraging factors for both domestic and foreign tourists. It is ironical to conceptualize the promotion of new varieties of tourism, including eco-tourism, circuit tourism, sports tourism, while the tourists from the outside world have to face huge obstructions to clear to visit the state.

It is interesting to note that most of political parties, barring the Congress, which conceptualized the implementation of activities under National Rural Employment Guarantee Act (NREGA), did not have well-thought plan of action to ensure employment generation. While talking to many of the youth in the Imphal city, soon after the election, it could be gathered that the employment generation pledge of the Congress motivated many of them to vote for the party.

Some of the issues such as the demand for declaring Jiribam and Sardar Hill as districts as articulated by the BJP, the NCP and the MPP, failed to get attention of other political parties.

It is important to note that the UNC stood for a uni-dimensional agenda carved around the issue of integration of the Naga inhabited areas of Manipur for the realization of the demand for 'Nagalim'. To the UNC and for that matter the UNDF nothing else seemed mattered.

It has been found that there are two broad issues that figured in the manifestos of various political parties. One was insurgency relate that included peace and conflict transformation in the state, demand for the withdrawal of the AFSPA and protection of human rights. The other was the broad issue of political stability for the development in all spheres of life in the state. A cursory view of the issues suggests that each and every developmental issue was linked with the need to form a stable government for which the state had been starving for four decades. While some of the parties, such as the Congress, put enormous emphasis on sustaining the current political stability of the last five years and promised to carry forward the development agenda further, the regional parties put forward the regional perspective of development. At any rate, the issues of development overshadowed other politically charged and volatile issues. It also appeared from media reporting that the public attention had been more on a performing government than on the unresolved issues of insurgency. For the people of Manipur, the development of the state in all fronts became the major issue, which sidelined the former. It does not mean that the issues centering round the question of peace, insurgency, presence of draconian laws and violation of human rights were relegated to obscurity. These were important issues, that would need more time to get resolved. Manipur could not wait to find these difficult issues resolved and then spring into action for all-round development of the state[11]. This dichotomy could be found in the campaign trail, as detailed in the next Chapter. There was also the valley-hill divide on the issue of territorial integrity of the state. The UNC's call for integration of all the Naga inhabited areas propelled the Meitei sentiment to protest. The door to door silent campaign, as stated in the next Chapter, indicates that for the electorate in the valley the issue of territorial integrity was very close to their hearts, while the UNC's issue to foster the cause of the NSCN became preponderant and pronounced in eleven hill constituencies inhabited by the Nagas. These two diametrically opposite issues had much impact, leading to the high turnout of the voters, who wanted to play a decisive role on these issues.

REFERENCES

1. *Imphal Free Press*, January 4, 2007
2. *The Sentinel*, February 2, 2007.
3. For details see *Imphal Free Press* and *The Telegraph*, July 16, 2004. Some of the NGOs distributed CD footage of the demonstration to score a point on the gravity of the situation in Manipur.

4. For details about Irom Shramila see O. Kulabidhu Singh, *Sharmila: A Mission for Peace* (Imphal: Oinam Ongbi Gulapmachu Devi, 2006) pp.71-74.
5. For details see *Report of the Committee to Review the Armed Forces (Special Powers) Act, 1958*, Government of India, Ministry of Home Affairs, 2005. The Report first appeared in a website www.hindu.com. The Executive Director of Human Rights Alert, Manipur, Babloo Loitongbam, published it in October 2006 and made it available for interested readers.
6. In a workshop organized by Peace Studies of OKDISCD in collaboration with the American Center, Calcutta, on March 24-25, 2006 at Imphal in which various civil society organizations including mutually hostile groups pleaded for the end of insurgency and the restoration of peace and order, for, the state had not gained anything except death and destruction as a result of prolonged spell of insurgency. For some details including a collection of original documents, see Anuradha Dutta and Ratna Bhuyan, *Genesis of Peace and Conflict in Northeast India*, Vol. I and II (New Delhi: Akansha, 2007).
7. http://www.icmr.mic.in/icmr/2005/April/0412pdf.
8. http://www.icmr.mic/inijmr/2005/April/0412.pdf
9. www.avert.org/indiaaids.htm
10. For some understanding of the Sixth Scheduled areas, see Rajendra Kshetri, *District Councils in Manipur: Formation and Functioning* (New Delhi: Akansha, 2006) and for the state of affairs in these are as during the colonial rule see C.G. Crawford, *Administrative Report, Manipur State*, in five volumes covering the period from 1922-1927 (Imphal: State Printing Press, 1923 to 1927).
11. The local dailies had been publishing the statements of the Chief Minister, who had been highlighting the government's priority to the task of development. Our own interactions with a number of political leaders, media persons, academicians led us to feel that they would pay greater attention to the development agenda so that Manipur could catch up with the

rest of the country. "Let the problem of insurgency continue and its other manifestations" commented a leading academic, who is also a political personality, "let also the developmental activities take their own course and speed. While the insurgency related matters might take time to find a solution, the development agenda should not take time for implementation. So, the voters have the natural choice to vote for development."

5

CAMPAIGN

Campaign is an organized effort which is to influence the decision making process within a specific group. In democracies, political campaigns often refer to electoral campaign, wherein representatives are chosen or referenda are decided.[1]

Campaign as a referral point in election politics denotes essentially a period when political parties try to reach out to the electorate, present their manifestoes and put forward their candidates and arguments in order to persuade them to vote for their candidates and parties.

In India, all political campaigns attract the general public. But election campaign in this country has always been a big crowd puller. It begins much ahead of the declaration of election schedule notified by the Election Commission India (ECI). The state of Manipur is no exception to it. The campaign for the 2007 Assembly elections began vigorously in the later part of 2006, when the three important issues figured in the public domain – viz, the demand for the repeal of the AFSPA, the territorial integrity of the state and the need to sustain the current political stability for the all-round development of the state. For example, Chief Minister Ibobi Singh organized a big show on December 6, 2006 to release a multi-colour booklet highlighting the achievements of the SPF Government during the uninterrupted tenure. It was an informal campaign in anticipation of the notification of the election dates. It was expected that any day the Election Commission of India would announce the dates through a formal notification. The Congress wanted to take an opportunity to start off the campaign, highlighting the achievements and the plans for future development of the state. Among the achievement on which he took the credit were proper and good management of the financial position of the state, conversion of the Manipur University into a central university, construction of railway line from Jiribam to Tupul, taking over the Kangla Fort complex from military occupation and so on.[2] However, other parties did nothing significant to the start informal campaign and waited till the announcement of the poll dates.

As soon as the notification of the Assembly elections was issued on December 29, 2006[3], the campaign gathered its natural momentum along with the organization of 'Political Conferences' or 'Political Conventions' by all the political parties, be it a national or a regional. The Congress, being the largest national party contesting in the state, called for a "Political Conference" at Imphal and organized 'Block Level Congress Committee Conference'. Similarly, all other national parties such as the BJP, the CPI, the RJD, the SP and the two regional parties, the MPP and the MSCP did not lag behind. They too went for the same exercise to make people aware of the importance of the elections and to secure the public sympathy and support. A typical conference/convention is a one-day but big affair in which all the leaders of each political party attend and make speeches highlighting the achievements of their party and criticizing the 'misdeeds and failures' of their opponents. In the midst of the festivity that marks such an event, the leaders outline the party's future plans and strategy to face the challenges put forward in the elections. This is an orchestrated prelude to serious campaign by the candidates after getting nominations from their respective parties.

The nomination process traverses a tricky and slippery path. For the top leaders, it is usually a foregone conclusion that they would get the nominations, but for the new aspirants and for some of the less reputed ones, there is no certainty. The new entrants in the election fray have to move from pillar to post, to impress the party hierarchy in order to get the nominations. It is a huge political battle to win.[4] At any rate, one would find that before the formal kicking off of campaign, there is a high drama of allotting party tickets to the candidates. Almost all political parties would try their best to select the potentially wining candidates from among those who applied for tickets, ignoring sometimes whether the selected person is a members of the party or not. This happened in respect of at least two political parties – the Congress and the MPP, which denied party ticket to veteran and sitting MLAs to accommodate new and inexperienced faces. Such drastic steps usually lead to violent response and change of party affiliation by the disgruntled persons; and they eventually join the election fray as rebel candidates. There were cases of block level workers resigning from the party's primary membership. A few such cases are cited below:

Case 1. Andro Block Congress Committee President Mansur Alam and hundreds of supporters resigned from the primary membership of the Party in protest against the party decision not to nominate their favourite candidate Thounaojam Shyam Kumar Singh to contest from the No. 7 Andro constituency understandably on the ground that he was arrested in New Delhi on October 2, 2006 along with two UNLF cadres allegedly for his links with the said insurgent fraction[5]. It may be mentioned that Singh contested from this constituency in 2002 with a Congress ticket but was defeated by Salam Chandra Singh by a margin of 1824 votes. This time the party looked for a new face. Consequently, he deserted the party and joined the MPP. The change of party affiliation brought rich dividend to him. He won defeating the Congress candidate.

Case 2. Elangbam Birmani, a sitting Congress MLA from 38 Hyanglam constituency was denied the party ticket. The nomination went to Elangbam Dwijamani Singh, a new face in the party. Biramani tendered resignation from the party along with some other party-members and supporters and joined the MPP.[6] This, however, did not alter the overall scenario of the party's prospect. The newcomer won the election defeating Biramani Singh.

Once the nomination affairs were over, the election wore a festive look in Manipur. The candidates started organizing large community or local feasts in their respective constituency. This is a time for the voters and especially the young voters to visit the residence of the candidates, who take every opportunity to woo them; then follows the formal campaign. In the case of the Assembly elections, 2007, almost all the political parties followed the routine campaign methodology by forming Election Committees at three levels – the Central Committee at the state level, the Local Committees at the district and constituency levels and the Ward Committees at the grassroots levels, each entrusted with specific campaign related responsibilities. While the Central Committee comprised the top leaders of the party, the other two were basically managed by the local level leaders and workers. The most important duty of the Central Election Committee was to supervise the whole effort including poster campaign, house to house campaign and campaign through public meetings. In addition to these, almost all the parties, including the Independents, constituted 'Development Committees' which took up the issues related to the development work in the constituencies, such as, construction and repair of roads and bridges, the drainage system in urban areas, development of market places and similar other works of public utility.

As in the past, the Election Committees organized local/leikai/cluster/ward and sagai (clan) meetings. They took the responsibility of organizing interactive camera meetings with small group of people (4/5 members) to be addressed by the candidate. In such meetings, the group narrated its problems and asked for monetary help. Such meetings are all followed by feasts.

It is noteworthy that despite the threat of the UNC not to campaign for the national political parties, compounded by possibilities of insurgency related violence, in which the workers and leaders including the candidates could be innocent victims, the usual practice of door to door campaign, also known as 'House to House Campaign', went on without any interruption.

It is true that the national parties, except the Congress, could not do much of it in the Naga inhabited areas. In the valley and other non-Naga hill constituencies, such campaigns went on unobstructed. It implied that the UNC call did not affect the normal electioneering. Such campaign may begin even before the election notification in some specific cases, but usually begins after the election notification or confirmation of the candidature. During this type of campaign all the candidates used to interact with the voters, and while doing so, they offer sweets, cigarettes, bidis, and in most cases money to those who were reportedly suffering from 'illness'. In one of such incidents, media camera captured a glimpse of Chief Minister Okram Ibobi handing over some money to an aged person, an act which tantamount to a breach of election code of conduct. There were allegations of distribution of thousand rupee notes amongst the voters by certain political parties. However, this grave accusation could not be verified, as no one, neither the distributor nor the recipient, would open mouth to tell the truth.

There were exceptions, for instance, Rajkumar Dorendra Singh, former Chief Minister of Manipur, who had been representing 14 Yaiskul constituency, contesting under the banner of the MPP, did not undertake house to house campaign, because of his age[7]. The task was taken over by his supporters and the party functionaries. But his abstention proved costly; it was one of the many reasons for his defeat in the last election.

It is interesting to note that for the first time there was extensive use of the Meitei script in the posters and banners of the regional parties, such as, the MPP and the MSCP in the valley constituencies presumably to win over the Meitei sentiment. It is noteworthy that there has been an emotional movement in the state in favour of the reintroduction of the Meitei script, replacing the Bengali one. On the other hand, the national political parties used mostly Bengali script in the campaign materials distributed in the plains, and the Roman script in the hill areas. They used English in the Naga and Kuki dominated areas; thus the hills-plains divide was strikingly visible. The UNC supported candidates invariably used English to reach out to the voters.

Campaign during the bandh

Manipur is one the states badly affected by the perennial problem of bandh calls given by various political parties and groups. However, during the 2007 electioneering period such a bandh had little impact on the campaign fever. There was only one 24 hour bandh call during this period given by the Kuki Student Organisation (KSO) on February 2, 2007 from 6 am to protest the death of a villager during a raid by security personnel on a church at Khoken Kuki Village in Senapati district. It was backed by Apunba Lup, which has been spearheading a campaign against the AFSPA and some other human rights group, including the Human Rights Alert and the Kuki Movement for Human Rights. However, it could not dampen the spirit of candidates and party workers, although all the establishments including business, in the capital city of Imphal were shut down.[8] The MPP was conspicuous in holding a massive rally at Patsoi constituency in the Imphal West District, which was made spectacular by pressing into service all types of vehicles that zipped in and out of the city. Other parties, of course, maintained a low profile in order to respect the sentiment of the organizers of the bandh. The bandh, of course, did not have any impact in the Naga dominated areas.

'Flag Hoisting' ceremony

The 'Flag Hoisting' ceremony is one of the most important ingredients of any election campaign in Manipur. It is a unique means to gather all the electorate under one umbrella and sensitize them about the importance of the elections, the party and the candidates. The ceremony is performed by almost all the contestant candidates cutting across party line. It is believed to be a journey for the contestants, to erect a new milestone in anticipation of possible win in the election.

The 'Flag Hoisting' ceremony is a traditional electioneering methodology. It has been in place in the election scenario in the past, but the trend and the contour are fast changing. In the previous elections, the ceremony was simple; it was a treated just as a formality to begin an election campaign of a candidate concerned. A simple function of hoisting the flag of the party of the candidate[9] with religious prayer and gifts (athenpot) of various items such as rice, vegetables and fruits from a few women party workers, and particularly, the voters of the candidate's home polling station, followed by a brief meeting in which the candidate used to deliver a speech. That was the order of the day in the past. Recent flag hoisting ceremonies have experienced a vast sea of change. Typically, a large procession is organized, in which thousands of voters in colourful dresses carrying large banners, coming from nook and corner of the constituency participate and shout slogans. This presents a festive look, and starts off the formal campaign. The procession is followed by large a band with a loud speaker describing the candidate's prospect. For the convenience of the participants, a number of vehicles are placed wherever necessary. Apart from this, athenpots are brought in large numbers from almost every ward/polling station. The first athenpot thinba party is followed by several others. Each party carries a head-load of gifts of all kinds of vegetables, fruits, rice, ghee and honey. This has been the tradition for many years. Athenpot thinba is performed by each contestant with religious fervour in all 40 Meitei dominated constituencies of the state. Now-a-days an election meeting is preceded by athenpot in which women voters take the lead. It has become a symbol of fund raising exercise.

The candidate has to treat her/his workers and supporters with tea and snacks, depending on her/his ability. The items offered as athenpot, such as rice and vegetables are often used to organize community feast. The candidates try to bring in as many supporters as possible to this function. This is a unique opportunity to show the numerical strength of the contestants. After all, election is a game of numbers. Whoever makes the whole show spectacular, with the presence of leading personalities in different fields, and with grandeur and good feast, steals the show. For such an expensive affair one needs huge fund. Here lies the vital question as to the democratic credibility of elections, which are weighed in terms of money power.

This is an occasion when the party leaders make lengthy speeches highlighting the achievements of the party, the failures and the misdeeds of the opponents and the promises to be redeemed after the elections. To cite a few examples may be relevant. As a mark of commencement of election campaign for the RJD, the state party President W. Nipamacha Singh, a former Chief Minister of Manipur, organized his 'Flag Hoisting' ceremony in his home constituency, Wangoi, on February 1, 2007 with an elaborate religious offering. The ceremony was following by a large public gathering in which he asked the voters to vote for the RJD and for his leadership. He promised that if his party came to power it would implement the Central Government pay commission recommendations for the government employees of the state. He also highlighted the achievements of Railway Minister and the RJD Chief Lalu Prashad Yadav. He accused the Congress of mis-governance and claimed that the Congress was supported by the underground outfits especially the NSCN (IM). He further claimed that the ministers and the MLAs in the SPF Government supported the NSCN (IM) by signing the declaration for integration of the Naga inhabited areas of Manipur under Nagalim.[10]

Star campaigners for various parties

The Congress

The Congress President and UPA chairperson Sonia Gandhi came to Manipur twice for election campaigning. Never in the past, had the Congress chief made two visits for electioneering. This is showed how seriously the party took the elections and tried to secure a comfortable majority in the 9th Assembly and form the government for the second consecutive term.

On the first leg of her election campaign, she visited Wangjing Kodompokpi ground in Thoubal; the home district of Chief Minister Okram Ibobi Singh, and addressed a huge public gathering on February 5, 2007. In her address, she dealt with three important issues and made categorical commitments. She reassured the people of Manipur that her party was committed to protect the territorial integrity of Manipur. She told the people that the Congress alone had the required will to stand by that commitment. Second, on the issue of the AFSPA, she said that the Congress had already lifted it from some constituencies in the Imphal valley and was considering the possibility of extending the withdrawal to other areas of the state. Third, she gave emphasis on political stability for an all-round development of the state, for which there was the need to return the Congress to power with a comfortable majority, for, to her it was only party that could provide a stable government in the state. In her speech, she put enormous emphasis on empowerment of women. Fourth, she applauded the role made by the womenfolk in various walks of life, more particularly, in the economy of the state. On insurgency, she called upon the youths of Manipur to shun violence and come forward for talks, as the doors were open for a constructive dialogue.[11]

On the second leg of her campaign on 12th February, she addressed public gatherings at Khoupum Lampak in Tamenglong District and at Tuibung peace ground in Churachandpur town. The contents of the campaign addresses remained almost the same, with reaffirmation of the commitment made on territorial Integrity of the state. This time, however, she skipped the reference to the issue of repealing or withdrawing the AFSPA but urged upon the insurgent youth to lay down arms and join the peace process in the state. She strongly advocated empowerment of women, particularly, in a state like Manipur where the women were front-runners in daily walks of life. She urged the people to vote for the Congress, designated the only party to fulfill any public commitment made to the people. She mentioned that the SPF Government in Manipur created a record in the history of Manipur, by completing its full five-year term for the first time in 40 years. She said: "The Congress has given a stable Government. This was possible with your support". The financial position of the state had remarkably improved. The Congress led SPF Government had already taken up various developmental projects, which the earlier Governments could not take up. She spoke on the need for peace for development of the state and reiterated the Prime Minister Dr. Manmohan Singh's call for dialogue with insurgent groups that would be carried forward to its logical conclusion. She reassured the people that the Congress party and the Union Government cared for the people of Manipur and that is why the UPA Government extended financial and other material support for the development of the state since 2004.[12] Sonia's visit to Tamenglong was considered as a reassurance to the voters that congress leaders – both in Delhi and Manipur cared for them. It was viewed by the public that Sonia Gandhi's second visit was a morale booster.[13]

Close on the heels of the campaign made by Sonia Gandhi, India's Prime Minister Dr. Manmohon Singh visited the trouble torn State of Manipur for an election campaign on February 17, 2007, just before the 3rd phase of polling covering mostly the constituencies in the Tamenglong District. Expressing happiness at the peaceful poll with heavy voter turnout, the Prime Minister stressed mainly on peace and stability, which were *sine qua non* to accelerate the pace of development in the state. The Prime Minister applauded the achievements that the Congress led Secular Progressive Front Government scored during the past five years. He was confident that given another five years, the Congress would ensure a brighter future of the state where there would be no poverty and illiteracy. He visualized Manipur as major producer of fruits like oranges, lemons and apples in the country and emerging as a leading tourist centre with its natural beauty. He put major emphasis on issues of tribal development, road linkage, better connectivity and agricultural production. He took the credit of transforming the Manipur University into a central university and thus changing the atmosphere of higher education in the state; he also spelt out the plan for a Manipur Institute of Technology and a Regional Institute of Medical Sciences. He emphasized that, given peace and stability a chance, one could develop the state into a mini Switzerland. He envisioned that Tamenglong District could be turned into a major centre for horticulture and tourism, if its natural resources were tapped.[14] Predictably, he maintained discreet silence on certain contentious issues such as territorial integrity of Manipur, the valley's opposition to the integration of all Naga-inhabited areas with Nagaland and the demand for repeal of the AFSPA. The purpose of the Prime Minister's visit to Tamenglong, was to boost the morale of the Congress workers and supporters, who could not campaign openly because of a diktat from UNC.[15]

The AICC General Secretary in charge the North East and Union Minister Oscar Fernandez, who is not new in the state, because of his frequent visits in connection with the peace processes in the region, also came to the state to join the election campaign. He was also fully involved in the process of nomination of the Congress candidates and the formal release of the party's manifesto, and he therefore, had made a prior visit for kicking off the election campaign. He was also present at the 'Flag Hoisting' ceremony of the party centrally organized in Imphal. He had a long stay and campaigned in the hill areas. He complained that some of his party candidates were unable to campaign freely in the hill districts because of threats from various armed groups.[16] Another Union Minister, P.R. Kyndiah, who holds the Ministry of Tribal Affairs also visited Churachandpur District on February 18, and participated in the District Congress Committee meeting held at the Community Hall and then addressed a press conference.[17]

It is noteworthy that the visit of the UPA Chairperson and the Prime Minister to campaign for the party, and particularly, the two visits of the party's star campaigner, Sonia Gandhi, generated unprecedented enthusiasm among the Congress workers, which eventually enhanced the prospects of the party to a great extent. No other party, including the BJP, could bring their star campaigner to do the job for the party candidates.

Members of the civil society participated in the public meeting at Moreh Town organized on behalf of the Congress candidate D.K. Korungthangtha; the gathering was addressed by Congress heavyweights like Oscar Farnandez, B.K. Handique, Major Ved Prakash, and K. Ranjit Govindas Konthoujam. It was attended also by a group of Maring Students Union, Maring Nupiya Langlam, Maring Uparup Assembly, Village heads and other community leaders of the town and Tengnoupal Assembly constituency.[18]

Chief Minister Okram Ibobi Singh, and Gaikhangam, the President of Pradesh of the Manipur Pradesh Congress Committee(MPCC), are the two most prominent election campaigners of the state unit of Congress. They were visible in all campaign meetings including the centrally organized in Imphal and other towns, as also in and the release of party manifesto. During the campaign the duo mostly highlighted the SPF government's achievements and the issues incorporated in the manifesto. It is interesting to note that they refrained from criticizing the diktat of the UNC not to campaign and vote for the national parties. Later, Gaikhangam ignored the UNC's call and said in a public meeting: "the diktat is nothing new. It has been going on for the past many years and we are immune to threats and intimidation now".[19] It is believed that the massive polling that took place on the first day of the election held on February 8, encouraged a similar turnout in the second phase. The Congress did not face any major threat or attack on it candidates and campaign activists. This had emboldened the party chief to make such safe and strong comments. Dr. T. Meiyna, the Lok Sabha MP from Inner Manipur Parliamentary constituency, was another prominent campaigner for the congress. In other words, the Congress had strength and resources to go for an all out campaign and could enlist the support of one and all of the higher echelon in the party.

It is also noteworthy that the Congress campaign did not suffer in the Naga dominated areas. The party was careful not to antagonize by undue massive fanfare in campaigning; in stead, it decided to undertake a silent door-to-door campaign, which proved effective in reaching out to the electorate. It was suspected that the Congress had an underhand deal with the NSCN (IM) to the effect that if it failed to get absolute majority it would form a coalition government with the support of UNC legislators.[20]

The MPP

Dr. Chandramani Singh , the President of Manipur people's Party(MPP) and former Deputy Chief Minister was a star campaigner for his party. He attended almost all the flag hosting ceremonies and public meetings of the party candidates. During the party campaign he spoke on various issues of peace and development, territorial integrity, scrapping the AFSPA and a host of other issues on economic and social development. He claimed that the MPP had become an umbrella organization of all the regional forces working for the welfare of the state with the result that it was in a position to expand its base dramatically. He was confident that with a new vibrant face the party would be able to win the election and form the next government in the State.

Okram Joy Singh was another prominent election campaigner of Manipur Peoples Party. He is a veteran leader of the party and proved to be an effective opposition leader representing the Langthabal Constituency since 2000 under the banner of the MPP. He is known to be an effective communicator in public meetings, and therefore, a crowd puller. While campaigning for the party he emphasized the positive dimensions of the party, which had now gained strength through the merger of the FPM; he lashed out the SPF for its failure on the economic front, law and order situation, and in the matter of withdrawal of the AFSPA. Besides campaigning in his own constituency, he campaigned in almost all other constituencies and a large meeting centrally organized by the party in Imphal. On this occasion, Th. Chaoba Singh, former Deputy Chief Minister, boasted that the newly christened MPP was a unique political platform, which could accommodate a number of leading figures. Calling himself as one of the 'Tin Murtis', other two being Chandramani and Joy Singh, he expressed deep satisfaction at the combined efforts of the MPP to win the confidence of the people and thus dislodge the SPF from power. He accused the Congress of playing minority and vote bank politics, while, in fact, not looking after the interests of the minorities; it never allowed a Muslim (Pangal) leader to become the Chief Minister of the state. On the other hand, he claimed, the MPP had been always taking up the problems of religious minorities and smaller communities. The MPP had elected Mohammad Alimuddin as the Chief Minister, soon after Manipur state was accorded full statehood.[21] This single instance testified to the secular credentials of the party.

Rajkumar Dorendro Singh, 72, a veteran political leader, who had been the Chief Minister for thrice and had a tenure as Rajya Sabha member contested from his home constituency, Yaiskul in Imphal East District as in the past. He was elected from this constituency for the first time in the 1974 Assembly election and had been representing the constituency since then, leaving just one break in 1995, when E. Kunjeshore Singh asked to contest. Despite his ill-health and inability to undertake door-to-door campaign in his own constituency, this former Chief Minister campaigned for the party in other constituencies and expressed confidence that his party would secure absolute majority in the Assembly and form the government.

It is noteworthy that there had been a whispering campaign against Rajkumar Dorendra Singh.[22] It was alleged that he was a corrupt and non-performing Chief Minister, who changed his party more than thrice and that joined the MPP with just only one objective to become the Chief Minister for the fourth time. It appears that this campaign, which indeed was strong, cost him and the party dearly. He lost the election in his home constituency and the party, too, suffered miserably.

The BJP

Rajnath Singh, the President of the BJP campaigned for the party. It contested in 14 seats, which was quite surprising. In the 2002 elections it contested 46 seats, the highest number of seats contested, since it entered in the election politics in Manipur in 1984. Out of 46 seats contested it could capture only four. The party had not been consistent in fielding candidates.[23] One of the BJP contestants explained to us the reason behind the party's decision to keep a low profile in the 9th Assembly elections. He said that the party did not dare to contest in the constituencies, where it did not have organizational infrastructure and where militancy had been visible. It was also haunted by the anger the Meitei people demonstrated when the Union the then Home Minister, L.K. Advani made a statement giving concession to the issue of 'Nalgalim'. It decided to contest in those constituencies where it had a bright prospect of winning. At any rate, Rajnath Singh landed on Imphal on February 2, 2007 and spoke on the issues of upholding and protecting the territorial integrity of the state, and on the demand for the repeal of the AFSPA and other related issues. Speaking on the economic backwardness of the state, he charged the UPA Government for its failure to check price rise, militancy in different parts of the country, farmers' suicide in Andhra Pradesh and Maharastra. He argued that insurgency was a law and order problem of the state, and blamed the SPF government for not bringing a political solution to it.[24]

Soon after the visit of Rajnath Singh, another star campaigner, Venkaiah Naidu, the Vice President and the former President of the party came to the state for campaigning. He participated in a public meeting at Leimakhong Bazar in the Saitu Assembly constituency on February 6, 2007. In his campaign speech, he accused the Congress-led SPF government of corruption and of laundering funds meant for development projects. He alleged that as result, the benefit of such central funds did not reach the common man, and also that a large sum of money had gone to the militant groups.[25]

Veer Satish, the BJP's General Secretary, looking after party affairs in the North Eastern region, was one of the stalwarts who campaigned in selected areas. In one of the press conferences organized by his party, he voiced an apprehension that the Congress might indulge in rigging in order to capture power for the second term. He branded the Congress-led SPF government as anti-people and accused it for not doing anything visible for the welfare of the people.[26] Some others such as Avinash Kohli, H. Borobabu Singh and M. Bhorot also campaigned for the party.

It is interesting to note that the BJP, which fielded only 14 candidates, stayed away from giving any challenge to the ruling SPF government. Therefore, it did not talk about the formation of government and its future agenda. The campaign remained confined to the polemics of accusation of the UPA government, and in certain cases, to highlighting the national agenda of the party. It appeared that the party gave a walk-over to the Congress in the matter of forming the next government. The result was terrible for the party as has been narrated in the next Chapter.

The CPI

The Communist Party of India (CPI) General Secretary A B Bardhan , visited Manipur on the eve election for campaigning and for releasing the party manifesto. During the manifesto release ceremony, the CPI leader proclaimed that no party would be able to form the next government, without the support of his party, as in the case of previous SPF government. He predicted a hung Assembly in which his party would play the role of a kingmaker. He proclaimed that the question of territorial integrity of Manipur was a non-negotiable issue on which his party would stand by the people of the state. He reiterated the demand for the repeal of the controversial AFSPA with immediate effect.[27]

The NCP

P A Sangma, the General Secretary of the NCP, a former Speaker of the Lok Sabha, and a known face in the region, campaigned for the party on various occasions. This time he made a hectic campaign, touring most of the constituencies where the NCP had been contesting. He made no concession in attacking the SPF government for its failure in many fronts such as law and order, economic development and the peace process. He expressed confidence that this time around the NCP would be the single largest party in the Assembly and would be able to form the government. He pledged that if the NCP forms the government on its own or with the support of like minded parties, the party would work for the economic development of the state and would work for the full implementation of the 'Look East Policy' in order to reap a high benefit out of it. He also promised that his party would withdraw the AFSPA from the state, generate employment opportunities and protect the territorial integrity of Manipur.[28]

Radhabinod Koijam, a former Chief Minister of Manipur, is another star campaigner of the NCP. He is a Mumbai trained lawyer and had a practice in Nagaland and continued for a while before throwing it all way for politics. He was elected from the Thangmeiband Assembly seat in 1980, as an Independent. Koijam joined the Congress later and retained his seat in the next two elections. He was made Deputy Chief Minister of the Rishang Keishing Government in 1995. In 2001, after the fall of W. Nipamacha Singh Government he became the Chief Minister.

The RJD

The RJD supreme, Lalu Prasad Yadav, the Union Railway Minister, could not make it come to Manipur to campaign for his party. It was a big setback for the state unit of the party. However, a host of national leaders, such as, the party's General Secretary and In-Charge of the North East, Harish Mahapatra, the Youth wing Secretary and Avinash Rai, the Youth wing President campaigned for the party vigorously. They spoke in the light of the promises made in the party manifesto. Significantly, all of them visited the state in the first week of the month when the campaign picked up; some of the leaders visited the troubled areas also.[29] All this had a definite impact on the prospects of RJD's candidates in a few constituencies.

The campaign made by other political parties such as the Lok Shakti Dal, the Janata Dal (Secular) and, for that matter, the SP and the CPI(M) did not have much impact, despite the fact that the top leaders of these parties visited to the state to campaign for their respective candidates. The visit of Ram Vilas Pashwan and the former Prime Minister, H.K. Deve Gowda, had little impact, as reflected in the miserable performance of these parties, failing to win even a single seat. (Chapter VI).

Campaign for the UNC sponsored Independent candidates

It all began with the UNC sponsored meeting held on January 16, 2007 in which all the Naga candidates, intending to contest in the 9th Manipur Legislative Assembly elections, assembled at Taphou Community Hall in Kangpokpi in Senapati District. As many as 60 aspirants attended the meeting. Besides the UNC, which took the lead in organizing the meeting, representatives of other organizations, such as, the All Naga Student Association of Manipur (ANSAM), the Naga People's Movement for Human Rights (NPMHR), the Naga Women's Union, Manipur(NWUM) and leaders of all Naga tribes attended the meeting. Some of the family members of the candidates were present and took part in the proceedings of the meeting.

The most striking note of the meeting was that all the 60 aspirants were asked to sign a declaration that demanded certain significant pledges from the signatories. To mention some of such pledges would be relevant. The declaration begins with a statement "I will fully support the Indo-Naga peace talks for a negotiated and honourable solution." One of the important points of the declaration goes like this: "I declare that I will accept, without any reservation whatsoever, the candidature of the particular person who is determined by the Naga people represented by the UNC to be the consensus candidate as per enunciated in the UNC's position paper in respect of constituencies of Manipur Legislative Assembly". Another declaration goes like this: "On being elected, I will steadfastly defend the interest of the Naga people for the integration and unification of the Naga areas." The declaration further mentions: "I will resign from Manipur Legislative Assembly if called upon to do so by the Naga people represented by the UNC." The declaration further states: "I shall not defect/split / merge to any political party or support any ruling government without the consent and approval of the Naga people represented by the UNC". The signing of the declaration was a show of solidarity of the Nagas under the banner of the UNC. The meeting was the starting point of the election campaign, which centered round the issue of the integration of the Naga areas under the broad framework of 'Nagalim'.[30]

The resignation of a few Naga sitting MLAs just before the expiry of the tenure of 8th Manipur legislative Assembly is a significant development in the nomination of the UNC sponsored candidates as also the strategy for campaign. The resignation of five sitting MLAs namely, PS Henry Paotei and Samuel Jendai of the FPM representing 47 Karong and 53 Tamenglong Constituencies, B.D. Bhering and Danny Shaiza of the BJP representing 41 Chandel and 44 Ukhrul constituencies, and Wungnaoshang Keishang of the MSCP representing 43 Phungyar, at the directive of the UNC was not unexpected. These MLAs had no option but to go by the UNC's call, mainly because of the fact that to retain their seats in the ensuing elections they had to enlist the support of the UNC. The Congress MLAs in the Naga inhabited areas, however, defied the diktat. It was also a campaign strategy to send a message to one and all how influential was this organization in the matter of election politics.

On January 19, 2007, the UNC brought out a list of eleven candidates on January 19, 2007 as its nominees to contest the 9th Manipur Legislative Assembly elections. These candidates formed an alliance, as stated in the preceding Chapter, called United Naga Democratic Front (UNDF) with a common flag and symbol. Under its banner the candidates spearheaded the campaign in the Naga inhabited areas. At the same time, it appeared that there was no fanfare in the campaign, unlike in the valley and other hill constituencies, where campaigning was a visible and spectacular affair. The reason behind this may be the fact that the UNC was complacent with success of its strategy of putting up consensus candidates, with NSCN(IM) backing.

Some of the prominent star campaigners for the UNC were Wungnaoshing Keishing, Danny Shaiza, Samuel Jendai and S. Kho John, who happened to be the convener of UNC.[31]

Poll Related Violence

Manipur had been experiencing poll related violence for a long time. No election could be conducted peacefully because of insurgency related and election boycott-related violence. The 9th Manipur Legislative Assembly election was no exception. There were pre-poll and post–

poll violence. Incidences of violence ranging from group clashes, arson in party offices, kidnapping of supporters and candidate, and armed attack leading to death, marred the elections. The Chief Electoral Officer of Manipur, R.R. Rashmi, claimed that Manipur was going to the polls with the heaviest ever deployment of security personnel in order make it peaceful and violence-free. Besides pressing the entire state security personnel into service, at least two units of central paramilitary forces had been deployed at each polling booth.[32] Even then violence took place as in the past. Some of such cases deserve attention.

The instances of kidnapping had been common during the whole period of electioneering. About 15 persons, including Anal Women Union Leader, Dr. Sameri Anal and social worker Morhing Lamkang were abducted by some unidentified armed miscreants in the Chandel District, soon after the first phase of the election. The motive and the forces behind the act could not be ascertained. But the incident rocked the district and the angry protesters blocked roads in different areas and submitted memoranda to the district officials, demanding immediate action to secure their safe return.[33]

The security forces detected an improvised explosive device at Uchiwa, just before Venkaih Naidu's addressed in an election rally on February 7 to campaign for H. Nikunja, who contested from the Mayang Imphal constituency. There was no major incidence of violence in Manipur up to the completion of the first phase of the poll that covered most of the Naga inhabited areas. Thereafter and before the final phase, there had been a series of violence of grave import; the deadliest one was triggered off on February 20, reportedly, by the UNLF in Ukhrul District.[34]

A day after the first phase of the election held on February 8, the Manipur People's Army, which is a military wing of the UNLF, ambushed a CRPF convoy that was escorting poll personnel and electronic voting machines. Three CRPF personnel, an election official and a civilian driver were killed.[35]

The most shocking incident was the kidnapping of an Independent candidate, Khangthuanang Panmei, who contested from the 53 Tamenglong constituency, reportedly by NSCN (IM) rebels.[36]

There were a number of incidences of violent activities, like firing the residence of candidates and at workers in different parts of Manipur. On the night of February 11, unidentified gunmen fired several rounds at the residences of a number of political workers at Sekmai in Imphal West District ostensibly to terrorize them on the eve of the second round of the poll.[37] Similar incidence of violence and intimidation occurred in Mayang Imphal and Naoriya Pakhanglakpa in Imphal West. In Heirangoithong, a Congress worker was gunned down a day ahead of the second phase of the poll. Unidentified gunmen targeted a presiding officer for allegedly distributing money among voters on behalf of a Congress candidate, Y. Erabot. Some assailants kidnapped the officer, L. Hemochandra, from Wangkhei constituency in Imphal West and charged him with distributing money on behalf of the said candidate; he was shot in the leg.

Group clashes erupted, following heated arguments between the supporters of the MSCP candidate,

K. Thamarjit and the Janta Dal (S) candidate, Thongram Tony. The supporters of Thamarjit were taking out an election rally when the supporters of Tony allegedly tried to stop them. Such incidents were considered to be normal and minor when compared with cases of kidnapping, gun firing and killing.

Soon after the first phase, there began a barrage of mudslinging among rival politicians,with greater intensity than before. The verbal assault vitiated electioneering atmosphere. Once partnership in the SPF had come to an end and the Congress decided to contest all but one seat, the honeymoon of two coalition partners also came to an obvious end. N. Mangi Singh, a CPI leader, accused Congress workers of kidnapping one of his men and lodged a complaint with the Chief Electoral Officer. There ensued a hate campaign between the two parties.

Here goes a brief survey of the incidences of violence.

1. N. Bhorot Singh (50), elder brother of N. Biren Singh, a sitting MLA and a Congress candidate contesting from Heingang Constituency in Imphal East was allegedly shot at by supporters of a rival candidate; this triggered a group clash at Luwangsangbam on February 15.

2. The UNLF claimed to have ambushed a convoy of security personnel at a place between Zoupi and Torbung at 1:10 pm in Chandel the same day i.e. February 15. However, no official confirmation was received so far.

3. The very next day of the last phase of polling phase, on February 24, sixteen security personnel belonging to India Reserve Battalion and Manipur

police were ambushed and shot dead at Ngarian Laimaton hill between Tamenglong and Bishnupur districts. These personnel were returning from Khoupum in Tamenglong District to Imphal after performing their security duty.

4. Samuel Jendai, a UNC sponsored Independent candidate, was attacked on February 21 by an unidentified gunman; he had a narrow escape from any injury.

5. Unidentified gunmen beat up nine Congress workers at 11:30 pm on February 8 at Wakhong Khuman of Nambol Assembly Constituency.

6. An incident of snatching away of Electronic Voting Machine from the polling station in ward no.5/6 of Kairao Assembly constituency took place on February 14, i.e. on the day of second phase of polling.

7. In a poll related violence, a Congress worker named Paokhulun Haokip of Saitu Assembly Constituency was shot dead by an unknown assailant at 11:30 pm on February 3 in Khulet village under Sapermaina Police Station.

8. At least one person was wounded and two vehicles belonging to Chief Minister O. Ibobi were damaged, when workers of the Congress and the MPP supporters of former Speaker, L. Jatra Singh clashed at Khangabok, around 8:00 pm on January 10.

When violence of any scale could be the order of the day in Manipur, with peace caged in chains for long, the above incidents seem almost a normal feature of any electioneering. These are not exceptions; besides the magnitude was reportedly not too serious, compared with what is experienced in the past.

Role of Media

Unlike his predecessors, the Chief Electoral Officer, R.R. Rashmi had made it a point to brief the media, twice a week, on the measures taken to conduct the polls smoothly and peacefully so that the voters could exercise their rights freely and without fear. He believed that free flow of information, disseminated through the print and electronic media, will remove fear and misgivings from voters' mind.[38]

The Manipur Information Centre, Delhi, a unit of the Department of Information and Public Relations, Government of Manipur, released a sixty (60) page 'Reference Handbook for Media' (Vol. I) on the 9th Manipur Legislative Assembly elections. The Handbook contains Manipur Profile, Manipur Election 2007 at a glance, press notes by the Election Commission of India (ECI) on December 29, January 5 and 10, map of Manipur showing Assembly constituency etc. This was done to sensitize the media along with others about the elections scheduled to take place in the state.

Both print and electronic media played a key role in disseminating election related information, news, advertisement and other features; there were heavy campaigns through media. The State Election Office formed a committee to look into campaign through media and to entertain applications for clearance of advertisements on television channels and cable networks by registered political parties having there headquarters in the state, as also all organizations and associations with registered offices in Manipur.[39]

Poknapham, a leading local Manipuri daily, took a lead in publishing certain election related features in its columns. Its "Karri Kendrada Kanana mai Pakkanni" (Which Kendra, Who Will Win) and another feature on women candidate- " Mapansuba Manipur Vidhan Sabhagi Mikhalda Miraep Oiriba Nupishing" (Women candidates in the 9th Manipur Legislative Assembly Election) which became quite favourite among the readers. The former made implied suggestions to the voters to elect the candidate of their choice in their constituency. In this column, the newspaper highlighted the candidates, the parties, previous achievements and their agenda for the future, so that the people could make a choice. The latter is all about women candidates, their political background and their perceptions about women issues and empowerment, gathered through interviews. This too, facilitated the voters in particular and readers in general to know about the women candidates.

Other print media such as *Sangai Exepress*, *Imphal Free Press*, *Yakairol* , *Naharol Thoudang*, *Huyen Lanpao*, and *Manipur Mail* played an impartial role. They published advertising materials of all the political parties contesting the elections, and provided ample space for advertisement. It appears that the print media played an impartial role, notwithstanding the fact that bigger parties bought larger space for party advertisements. The media appears to have focused, with importance, on issues such as demand for the repeal of the AFSPA, territorial integrity of Manipur and economic development of the state.

Electronic media too played its role in the election campaign. Information Service Television Network (ISTV), a prominent and a most favourite private sector television network gave adequate coverage on the elections, parties and candidates with a fair deal of impartiality. All India Radio broadcast from Imphal, carried campaign features of the constesting political parties. A special programme, with specific time frame, was allotted to the political parties to highlight their manifesto and issues. Being a government establishment it maintained its obvious impartiality.

Militant Groups during the campaign

Most of the militant groups played their role on expected lines, during the electioneering period, from December 20 till the end of the third phase of the elections. The UNLF openly boycotted all the national parties and supported the regional parties and independent candidates. In the valley it maintained a low profile due to heavy deployment of security personnel. But in the hill areas its campaign, accompanied by violence, was intense and terrifying, as a result of which most of the national parties could not do much campaigning. The Independents, however, did not face any major threat, and consequently, could continue their campaign without hindrance.

The Revolutionary Peoples Front (RPF), a banned insurgent group, boycotted Prime Minister's visit to the state on February 18, with a call for general strike from 6 am in the morning for 12 hours. Yet, the people came out in large numbers to attend the meeting addressed by the Prime Minister.

It is a known fact that the NSCN (IM) supported and backed the Independent candidates sponsored by the UNC. There are also reports of a call issued by the NSCN(IM) to boycott the last phase of polling scheduled for February 24, in which 12 constituencies in four districts, namely Churachandpur, Chandel, Jiribam and

Tamenglong were covered. Out of these, half of the constituencies are Kuki dominated. The NSCN (IM) call was reportedly motivated by its design to immobilize the Kuki electorate. Therefore, it called for a curfew from 7 am to 4:30 pm on the polling day with a design to keep the Kuki voters away from voting in 52, 53 and 54 constituencies. There were also whispering threats in the villages of Tamenglong from organizations to vote for their desired candidates, and to keep away the supporters of Khanthunang Panmei, who was not a NSCN (IM) favourite, and was abducted, reportedly, by the NSCN (IM).[40]

The Congress candidate S.T. Kohring Anal and sitting MLA B.D. Behring (Independent) opted out of the fray because of alleged threats from armed persons. The CPI's candidates in Chandel and Tamenglong constituencies were also forced to stay away from the race. In the midst of threats, three Kuki candidates of Tengnoupal constituency in Chandel District decided to work for only one consensus Kuki candidate, Haopu Haokip of MPP, to defeat the Naga candidates in the constituency.. Onjamang of CPI and Jamkholet of Samajwadi Party, supported Chungsei of the RJD.

Suspected NSCN-K issued a diktat in Zeliangrong region banning all candidates from participating and campaigning in the elections. It took strong exception to an incident in which an Independent candidate, Khanthunang Panmei was made to sign, under duress, an apology to the NSCN (IM) leader Kilonser. It raised questions as to why NSCN(IM) and the UNC should campaign only for Samuel Jendai and ban others from doing the same for their respective parties and candidates. It argued that such highhandedness was not acceptable to the people of Zeliangrong.[41] To express its anger, its cadres opened fire on the security guards of Samuel Jendai in Duilun area of Tamenglong. It asked the electorate of Tamenglong not to support any candidates belonging to the NSCN (IM) for its "dictatorial activities".[42]

The Kuki militant groups, such as, the KRA and the KNF are believed to have supported some candidates directly or indirectly.

The Peoples United Liberation Front (PULF), a Muslim based militant group found to have engaged itself in the election campaign directly or indirectly. They were active in some Muslim dominated areas and in some constituencies, where the Muslims have a sizeable population. They operated in Thoubal district, and especially in Wabagai Constituency. They extended support to the Congress candidates in some constituencies, and to the MPP in others.

It is interesting to note that other militant groups such as the United National Liberation Front (UNLF), the Kanglei Yayol Kanna Lup (KYKL) and The People's Revolutionary Party of Kangleipak (PREPAK) made it a point to use the electioneering environment to further their campaign against Tipaimukh dam.

Manipur CPI Secretary B.B. Sharma, in a memorandum to Governor Dr. S.S Sidhu, demanded free and fair polling in the third and final phase in the state on February 23. He drew the attention of the Governor to the deterioration in law and order situation and alleged that some militants had threatened the voters during the first phase of polling on February 8 and prevented some of them from voting. Threats were issued to CPI candidates and their workers by restoring to rampant shooting and by exploding hand grenades near their houses. He alleged that the armed militants also distributed live bullets to the workers of his party asking them not to work for their candidates. On the eve of third phase of polling, underground militants forced two CPI candidates in Chandel districts to retire, he claimed.[43]

The 4000 strong Kuki electorate in a cluster of 31 nondescript villages, straddling Chandel and Tengnoupal Assembly Constituencies along the Indo-Myanmar border, issued a statement saying that they would not venture out to vote. That did not mean that they were boycotting the elections. They would miss the poll simply because it was not safe to venture out of their villages. The Kuki Movement for Human Rights said that all paths leading to these villages and even to the paddy fields were strewn with mines. S. Chongloi, Vice-Chairman of the rights panel said almost 35 – 40 square kilometers across these villages have been mined by the militants to prevent security forces from raiding militants' hideout along the border.

There are allegations that security forces also planted mines in the area to keep the militants at bay. It was impossible to verify the authenticity of such claims and counter claims.

Role of Civil Society

The UNC is a prominent Naga based civil society organization, which engaged itself directly in the poll process by selecting, campaigning for and funding the candidates in 11 constituencies. Its main objective, as stated in an earlier context was to furnish for a strong voice in favour of integration of all Naga inhabited areas under 'Nagalim'.

The Meitei National Front (MNF), a valley based Meitei civil society group, extended full support to the MPP. In a statement which appeared in both print and electronic media, it declared that the party stood for the cause of their people and territorial integrity of Manipur. Expressing its strong commitment to the cause of regionalism and to the ethos of the people living in the state, it declared that in its opinion that the MPP alone would be able to protect the interests of the Meitei people and that is why it would support and campaign for them. It formed a committee of seventy called "Election Camp Committee" to work for the party.[44]

The Meira Paibi[45] was found to be engaged in the election campaign, though not under its banner. Its leaders campaigned for the MPP candidates. It is interesting to note that in spite of its being an all-women organization, it did not campaign for any woman candidate. It, however, staged a sit in demonstration on February 16, in front of the headquarters of the Imphal West District, to protest against the incidents of poll-related violence in which innocent civilians became easy targets and urged the authorities to ensure security. Coinciding with this, more than 3,000 women took out a 20 km long march on that day in Zaliangrong to protest against reported threats and intimidation by supporters of the UNC and to demand free and fair election. The march was organized by the Zeliangrong Women's Union. The president of the Union, Mazatliu Gangmei and the secretary, Adim Kamei, submitted a memorandum to the district electoral officer, after the march and urged him to ensure adequate arrangement for a peaceful poll so that voters could exercise their right, without fear and intimidation.[46] Similar protest had been registered in Tamenlong and Chandel Districts on February 21 organized by women activists to protest against the UNC's diktat and acts of violence.

It appeared that these demonstrations organized by various civil society organizations and voice of protest against the acts of violence reportedly indulged in by the UNC, particularly the abduction of Anal women Union Leader Dr. Sameri Anal and social worker, Morhing Lamkang, and 15 others, received huge support from a broad cross section of voters. They expressed anger by defying the poll boycott call in certain places. All this proved costly to the UNC sponsored candidates.

In a significant move soon after the notification of the elections, the All Manipur Anti Drug Association (AMADA), a civil society organization, working for the protection of people against drug and alcohol, called for a ban on the use of any narcotics and drugs including alcohol during the election campaign. It harshly warned that any candidate found to be guilty of indulging in use of drugs and alcohol would be socially boycotted and would not be voted for.[47] Some of the militant organizations too issued such warnings. Consequently, it appeared that no candidate could take recourse to distribution of alcohol, not to speak of drugs, to voters during the long campaign period.

The Manipur Assembly elections, 2007, experienced a long phase of campaign for about two months beginning with its notification on December 29, 2006. The campaign was marred by violence, which had been a regular feature in the state. It was not unusual in a state where violence and civil life go together. The most striking point to be noted is that even in the midst of violence, intimidation, poll boycott call and the UNC's diktat to bar the national parties from electioneering, more than 80 per cent people exercised their franchise. This emphatically shows that the spirit of democracy cannot be stifled by violence.

REFERENCES

1. http//en.wikipedia.org/wiki/political-campaign.
2. "CM sings 'good performance' report card" *The Sangai Express*, December 7, 2006.
3. *ibid*, December 30, 2006.
4. An attempt was made to study the nomination process of leading political parties. But it was impossible to consult the proceedings of the parties to find out what factors played the most crucial role in the nomination process. Interviews with some of the political leaders did not give any clear picture. Yet it could be surmised that a few factors such as incumbency, money power, reputation as dedicated party worker and closeness to the top leaders were key factors that decide the fate of aspirants in getting party tickets.
5. Thounaojam Shyam Kumar was arrested in New Delhi before the poll but he contested to win with a record margin. This will be elaborated in the next Chapter. For details of his arrest see *Thoudang*, October 3, 2006.
6. For details see *Poknapham*, January 15, 2007.
7. *The Telegraph*, February 12, 2007.
8. *ibid* and *The Sangai Express*, February 3, 2007
9. In the case of the Independents, any symbolic flag is hoisted.
10. *Naharol Thoudang*, February 2, 2007.
11. For details of Sonia Gandhi's speech see *Pokhnapham and Imphal Free Press*, February 6, 2007.

12. Sonia Gandhi's speech in three places had been given wide coverage in all the local newspapers such as *Imphal Free Press, Pokhnapham* and *Sangai Express* and in a national daily, *Telegraph*, February 13, 2007.
13. *Telegraph*, February 16, 2007.
14. For details of Dr. Manmohan Singh's speech see *Sangai Express, Imphal Free Press* and *Telegraph*, February 18, 2007.
15. *Imphal Free Press* and *Telegraph*, February 19, 2007.
16. *Telegraph*, February 2, 2007.
17. *Sangai Express*, February 19, 2007.
18. For details see *Poknapham*, February 17, 2007.
19. *Telegraph*, February 16, 2007.
20. A few academics, media personalities and political activists hold this view. They also argue that this unwritten agreement enabled the Congress to campaign freely in those areas. This is the reason for which the UNC had failed to achieve its objective of returning all the eleven candidates of its choice.
21. *Poknapham*, February 3, 2007.
22. Based on the information gathered through interview with media persons, social activists and academic persons who preferred to remain anonymous.
23. For some details see the tables inserted in Chapter III.
24. *Poknapam*, February 3, 2007.
25. *ibid,* February 7, 2007.
26. *ibid,* February 16, 2007
27. *ibid,* February 22, 2007
28. *ibid,* February 4, 6 and 21, 2007.
29. *ibid,* February 7, 2007
30. For details see *Poknapham*, January 17, 2007.
31. For details see *Imphal Free Press*, January 17-20, 2007.

32. *Telegraph*, 8 February 2007.
33. *Imphal Free Press*, February 21, 2007.
34. *Telegraph*, 21, February 2007.
35. *Imphal Free Press* and, *Telegraph*, February 10, 2007.
36. For some details see Chapter VI.
37. *Sangai Express*, February 12, 2007.
38. *Telegraph*, February 21, 2008.
39. *Imphal Free Press*, January 13, 2007.
40. *Poknapham*, February 23, 2007.
41. *Sentinel*, February 22, 2007.
42. *Telegraph*, February 22, 2007.
43. *Imphal Free Press*, February 21, 2007.
44. For details see *Imphal Free Press* and *Poknapham*, February 1, 2007.
45. Literal meaning is women torch bearers. Traditionally, women carry torch at night to keep vigil against any intruders and for safety and protection of the people. Now it is a women civil society organization actively engaged in civil rights movements. It organized the naked demonstration in front of the Kangla Fort on July 15, 2005 to protest against the killing of Manorama Devi. Critics of the organization say that its front rank leaders are the mothers of some insurgents, therefore, it represents, among others, the sentiments of such groups.
46. *Telegraph*, February 17, 2007.
47. See *Sangai Express*, December 31, 2006.

6

DECISIVE TURNOUT AND MANDATE

A clear mandate in elections has increasingly become elusive in the electoral process in India both at the national and the states levels. Consequently, politics of coalition has become the order of the day.[1] The monopoly of one party rule was effectively challenged by various assertive political groups. Consequently, single party domination at the Center has now become a daydream ever since the end of the Congress rule at the Centre in 1996. In a number of states, the coalition experiments have proved to be working successfully, despite occasional hiccups. In certain states, coalition means political instability and frequent change of governments; Manipur falls under that category as detailed in Chapters I and III. The Assembly elections of 2007 have thrown away the burden of fractured mandate and brought the Congress to power, with a clear mandate to govern the state for next five years. It happened after 40 years of instability and uncertainty. The heavy turnout of the electorate made the mandate decisive and spectacular.

Despite the threats issued by the militant groups against the national parties, five major national parties—the BJP, the CPI, the CPI(M), the Congress and the NCP - joined the election fray. As many as 8 State parties, 5 registered but not recognized parties, also fielded their candidates. In other words 18 political parties were in the race, besides 55 Independents. In total, 308 contestants were in the election battle. As in the past, election fever gripped the valley as well as the hills of Manipur. The turnout, as expected was high, though lower than that of 2002 by 3.65%, but still significantly high with 86.73 per cent out of which the female votes (86.82%) were higher than the male counterparts (85.88%). The first phase of the election held on February 8, 2007 set the mood of the electorate whose turnout (88.95%) was a spectacular demonstration of faith of the overwhelming majority in parliamentary democracy. As stated in Chapter III, the first phase covered most of the sensitive constituencies, where the UNC had a strong hold. The speculation was that the UNC supported candidates would sweep the elections in all the 11constituencies, where it had stakes in political and demographic terms.

The heavy turnout in the first phase had a direct impact on the second phase, which covered most of the valley constituencies, predominantly inhabited by the Meiteis. As stated in Chapter IV, the key issue that divided the Naga dominated hills and the Meitei inhabited plains is that of the question of integrity of Manipur. The strategy of some section of the Naga electorate was to return all the 11 UNC sponsored candidates in order to make the voice favouring Nagalim strong on the floor of the Manipur Assembly. By implication, it invited a befitting response from the valley constituencies; the heavy to turnout on the voting day, February 14, resoundingly in favour of the party that, understandingly, could protect the Meitei interests. Things moved on expected lines. There was an equally heavy turnout on the day of the second phase of polling. All this made the third and the final phase slated for February 23 easy and resounding. The political consciousness among the voters was not only reflected in terms of heavy turnout but in the least instances of invalid voting, for, only 373 votes (0.03) were found invalid.

The message was loud and clear. The people of Manipur have demonstrated once again, as in the past, their strong faith in the elections held under the provisions of the Constitution of India. The secessionist forces, too joined the fray, and by implication, registered their allegiance to the Constitution and its operative mechanism. There are other notable significances of the election results, which need elaboration and analysis.

It is important to have a glance over the election results, in terms of party performance (Table 6.1). The most striking was the Congress return to power, on its own after a gap of 40 years. As in 1967, it captured 30 out of 60 seats in the Manipur Assembly. None others could reach the double figure. All total, 13 parties scored duck. Independents captured 10 seats out of which 6 were UNC supported candidates.

It is noteworthy that the percentage of votes polled by the national parties in 2007 elections (58.17) was much higher than that of the regional parties in Manipur (22.42). It is a clear indication of the weak foundation on which regional parties stand. The only party, which could muster a two-digit percentage of votes, was the MPP (15.45). As already stated in Chapter III, the regional parties could not make a spectacular performance, in any of the elections in the state. It is not a difficult task to figure out the reasons for the failure of regionalism in Manipur in view of regionalism cohabitating in a divided house. A host of factors such as frequent shift of allegiance of the regional leaders from one party to another damaged the image of the parties. Leaders like Dorendra Singh or Rishang Keishing changed parties for more than thrice with the sole intention of becoming the Chief Minister. Other contestants too did not stand on exception, as will be revealed in the following section which deals with the voting trend in 12 constituencies, presented here as case studies. It is found that inconsistency of leaders impaired their own, as also the party prospects.

Table 6.1
Party-wise performance in the Assembly elections, 2007

Sl. No.	*Party*	*Seats contested*	*Seats won*	*% of votes polled*	*% of votes in seats contested*
1	BJP	14	0	0.85	3.95
2	CPI	24	4	5.97	15.07
3	CPI (M)	1	0	0.08	6.45
4	Congress	59	30	34.30	35.24
5	NCP	27	5	8.58	20.90
6	AIFB	2	0	0.01	0.26
7	JD(S)	2	0	0.48	17.62
8	JD(U)	3	0	0.29	6.69
9	LJP	19	0	1.50	4.85
10	MPP	36	5	15.45	26.29
11	RJD	28	3	6.67	15.08
12	RSP	1	0	0.05	3.00
13	SP	20	0	0.90	2.62
14	MSCP	6	0	1.86	19.84
15	NNLP	1	0	0.05	2.57
16	NPP	5	3	3.46	42.90
17	PDA	1	0	0.10	9.67
18	SAP	4	0	0.07	0.88
19	Independents	55	10	19.51	39.63
20	Total	308	60	100	

Source: Election Commission of India

Close on the heels of the argument that regionalism has hardly any future in Manipur, one could comfortably hypothesize that the Assembly elections in 2007 had given a decisive mandate on two issues. The first is the rejection of the concept of Nagalim even in the Naga inhabited areas. In all the Naga dominated constituencies the issue was a major political plank. The UNC worked hard to get all the 11 "Independent" candidates of its choice to win and eventually raise the Nagalim issue on the floor of the Assembly in a formidable manner. It could manage to elect only six. In a constituency like Tamenglong, the Naga candidate was defeated by a non-Naga candidate. In four others such as Saikul, Karong, Saitu and Nungba, the UNC supported candidates lost the elections. According to Gangmumei Kamei,[2] the elections of 2007 "was a kind of referendum" against the issue of Nagalim and for the territorial unity and integrity of the state Manipur.

Second, to most of the scholars, journalists and political personalities whom we interviewed soon after the elections, the 2007 elections rejected decisively the idea of a sovereign state of Manipur and accepted the merger of the state with the Union of India 58 years back as a *fait accompli*. The fact that in the 2007 elections too, as in the past, the heavy turnout on the days of elections throughout the length and the breadth of the state, was an unequivocal message to one and all, that reversion to the pre-1949 position is a daydream.

Another crucial issue was the demand for the withdrawal of the AFSPA. The issue fizzled out when campaign started. The verdict for the Congress and the percentage of votes polled by the national parties could be safely treated as a clear suggestion that the demand for the withdrawal of the controversial Act had little impact on the outcome of the election results, despite the fact the issue is still alive and the human right groups have carried on a sustained campaign against its retention.

One crucial revelation of the 2007 elections is that the Meira Paibi has hardly any hold among the electorate in the state. It is true that the women turnout surpassed the males, as already stated, but failed to elect a single woman candidate. The sitting woman legislator, Wahengbam Leima Devi, the lone representative from the women electorate, was defeated by her long time rival R.K. Anand (Table 6.5). Our interviews with a number of scholars, journalists, political personalities and activists suggests that in a society essentially dominated by patriarchy, woman torch bearers have hardly any space of influence in the political decision-making and participating structures.

It was not intriguing that the Congress could steal the show in the highly competitive politics, understood in terms of election fortune. In the preceding Chapter, it was argued that the nature of the campaign of the Congress party was matchless when considered from the perspective of grandeur exhibited on the 'Flag Hoisting Day": the visits of the national leaders and the door to door campaign, compared with other parties – both regional and national. Although the allegation, that it was more a show of money power than people's support, was tagged with the Congress campaign, the visibility of the party's massive presence in all the constituencies and the hard work done to secure votes was loud and clear. At any rate, one tends to ask the obvious question - what are the reasons for the Congress victory? The victory was spectacular in several ways. To improve its position from 20 seats in the outgoing Assembly to 30, and to raise its support base from 27.62 per cent to 34.30 was indeed a remarkable feat. The victory of the Congress exposes the weakness of the opposition parties - both national and regional. It also speaks of the shift of the support base from the non-Congress to the Congress in large a number of constituencies. The Congress snatched as many as 17 seats from the opposition. Table 6.2 details the situation. In most of the cases the margin was big, and therefore, statistically significant. The Congress retained 13 out of 20 seats. Only in one constituency named 59 Saikot, it suffered erosion. In all other constituencies, the party enjoyed significant increase in the voters' support. In the Saikot constituency the party faced a stiff opposition from the NCP because of which it could secure 13,010 votes as against 16,699 polled in 2002. It was a case of anti-incumbency, a lesson to the less functioning and complacent sitting MLA who took it for granted that once elected, he was destined to win all elections. The combined regional parties under the banner of MPP had failed to alter the situation to its advantage. The most notable reason for the failure is that the common voters suspected the political steadfastness and integrity of the leaders of the MPP. Most of them had to face the charge that they were compulsive floor-crossers and deserters. Once the credibility of the leaders of a united forum is severely defaced, it becomes an uphill task to restore the honour.

The FMP was the main victims at the hands of the Congress. It lost 8 seats to the Congress out of its 13 incumbents. The Congress too suffered setback in 11 constituencies where it could not retain its hold (Table

6.3). It had to concede defeat to four Independents supported by the UNC, 2 RJD, and 2 MPP candidates. The swing in the choice of the electorate went against the BJP, which not only failed to retain its 4 seats in the last Assembly, but drew a blank this time. The over all percentage of votes polled by the BJP fell from 9.59 to 0.85 and from 12.11 in the seats contested to 3.94. The FPM, too, suffered along with allies such as the MPP despite its unified fight under the common banner of the latter. In the 2002 elections, the FMP secured 13 and the MPP 2 seats; this time the combined efforts could bring fortune to only 5 candidates. To state succinctly, the Congress was the real gainer and all others, losers. The UNC candidates expected to sweep in all the 11 constituencies; could manage to secure 5 seats only.

Table 6.2
Constituencies snatched by the Congress from other parties in 2007

Sl. No	*Constituencies*	*Congress candidates*	*Winning parties, 2002*
1	11 Sagolband	Dr. Khwairakpam Singh	MNC
2	12 Keisamthong	L. Jayanta Kumar Singh	FMP
3	13 Singjamei	Irengbam Hemchandra Singh	FMP
4	14 Yaiskul	Elangbam Kunjeswar Singh	BJP
5	15 Wangkhei	Yumkham Erabot Singh	MSCP
6	18 Konthoujam	Dr. S. Budhichandra Singh	DRPP
7	23 Mayang Imphal	Dr. K. Ratan Kumar Singh	FMP
8	27 Moirang	M. Manindra	FMP
9	28 Thanga	T. Mangibabu Singh	FMP
10	31 Thoubal	Okram Ibobi Singh	FMP

(Contd...)

Sl. No	*Constituencies*	*Congress candidates*	*Winning parties, 2002*
11	32 Wangkhem	K. Meghachandra Singh	MPP
12	33 Heirok	M. Okendro	FMP
13	34 Wangjing Tentha	M. Hemanta Singh	CPI
14	37 Kakching	Y. Surchandra Singh	CPI
15	38. Hiyanglam	E. Dwijamani Singh	NCP
16	47 Karong	D.D. Thaish	FMP
17	57 Henglep	T. Manga Vaiphei	SAP

Source: Election Commission of India

Table 6.3

Parties which snatched seats from the Congress in 2007

Sl. No	*Constituencies*	*Winning Candidates*	*Parties*
1	21 Naoriya Pakhanglakpa	R.K. Anand	MPP
2	30 Lilong	Md. Helaluddin Khan	RJD
3	36 Wabgai	Dr. Deben Singh	CPI
4	45 Chingai	Dr. Khashim Ruivah	Independent
5	46 Saikul	Doukhomang Khongsai	NCP
6	48 Mao	M Thohrii	Independent
7	49 Tadubi	K. Raina	Independent
8	51 Saitu	Haokholet Kipgen	MPP
9	52 Tamei	Awangbow Newmei	Independent
10	55 Tipaimukh	Ngursanglur	RJD
11	56 Thanlon	V. Hangkhanlian	NPP

Source : Election Commission of India

As in the past, this time too the women candidates failed miserably. None of the twelve candidates could come out victorious. Even the sitting MLA, Wahengbam Leima Devi of the Congress, had to face defeat at the hands of R.K.Anand of the MPP.

It will be necessary to take up a few constituencies for an in depth analysis so that a clear picture emerges. The 1974 Assembly elections, and not the 1972 elections, could be treated as a base point. The number of and the names of the constituencies have been finally fixed at the time of 1974 elections, and therefore, it is convenient to take 1974 as the base year. It would enable to have a clear picture of the trend in the elections of certain important constituencies and present an overview of the election politics in the state.

A Few Case Studies

(1) Number **14 Yaiskul** is one of the important Meitei dominated general constituencies for the reason that it was held by the former Chief Minister of Manipur Rajkumar Dorendra Singh since 1974 except for five years (1995-2000) when he decided to stay away from the election fray. Table 6.4 shows that he had considerable hold in the constituency, quite naturally for the reason that he had been thrice the Chief Minister of the state. He became the Chief Minister for the first time in December 1974 and continued in office till May 1977. He was appointed the Chief Minister for the second time in January 1980 for a brief span of 11 months. The third tenure was also short but was slightly longer than the previous two (April 1992 to December 1993).

Table 6.4
Voting trend in 14 Yaiskul constituency since 1974

Year	*Votes polled by the winner*	*Votes polled by nearest rival*	*Difference*
1974	R.K.Dorendra Singh 3319 (MRP) 36.75%	Hawaibam Nilmani Sing 2935 (Congress) 32.50 %	384
1980	R.K. Dorendra Singh 4609 (Congress) 42.53%	Ayekpam Birmangol Singh 2744 (JP) 25.32%	1865
1984	R.K. Dorendra Singh 5157(Congress) 42.74%	Ayekpam Birmagol Singh 2796 (IND) 22.96%	2361
1990	R.K. Dorendra Singh 6708 (Congress) 42.56%	Elangam Kunjeswar Singh 5047 (JD) 32.02%	166
1995	Elangam Kunjeswar Singh* 5932 (BJP) 36.39	Gurumayim Joykumar Singh 5461 (MPP) 33.50%	471
2000	R.K. Dorendra Singh 9798 (BJP) 51.52%	Elangbam Kunjeswar Singh 9221 (MSCP) 48.48%	577
2002	R.K. Dorendra Singh 8107 (BJP) 45.01%	Elemgbam Kunjeswar Singh 6981 (Congress) 38.76%	1126
2007	Elangbam Kunjeswar Singh 11567 (Congress) 59.89%	R.K. Dorendra Singh 7321 (MPP) 37.90%	4246

* Rajkumar Dorendra Singh did not contest

Source: Election Commission of India

The figures in the Table tell in unmistakable terms that Rajkumar Dorendra Singh had always been a winner till 2007 and used to secure impressive percentage of votes. Why did he fail to retain his hold and why did the voters this time shift their favour to inflict a decisive defeat on him? There were two major allegations leveled against him during the electioneering. Despite the fact that he had been the Chief Minister more than once, he failed to make a mark in matters of governance in the state. The second allegation was more lethal. He changed political affiliation more than four times. He won his first election battle in 1974 with the MPP ticket. Opportunist as he was, it is alleged, he took no time to change his party to join the Congress; later he shifted to the BJP when it was ruling party at the Centre. Now after the 2004 Lok Sabha polls with the BJP in doldrums, he once again changed his party - this time to the conglomeration of regional groups and parties under the banner of the MPP. The campaign against him on the two counts was too strong for R.K. Dorendra Singh to counter. It led to his defeat by a huge margin in a four-cornered contest. It was essentially a straight battle between R.K. Dorendra Singh and the Congress candidate Elangbam Kunjeswar Singh. The other two candidates – Huidrom Badankumr Singh (RJD) and Jagdish Sharma (Independent) – who lost their security deposits, could manage to get 356 and 69 votes respectively. It is noteworthy that the erosion of Dorendra Singh's support base was not alarming, for, there was a loss of 786 votes this time compared to the figure he polled in 2002. But the margin of defeat was quite considerable, 4246 votes. It is noteworthy that there was no BJP candidate in the constituency. It appears that the BJP supporters preferred to cast their votes in favour of the Congress candidate rather than for Dorendra Singh, who had deserted the party at a difficult hour.

(2) **21 Naoriya Pakhanglakpa** constituency, a male dominated one, shot into prominence in 2000 by electing a woman candidate for the first time. Wahengbam Leima Devi, an Independent candidate, wife of a former three times MLA and also Rajya Sabha member, W. Angou Singh, won the election defeating Akoijam Ibobi of SAP by a margin of 1702 votes. An educated woman with BA and BT degrees, she was known as a social worker. There was heavy turnout of the voters to the tune of 92.33 per cent. This is one of the largest constituencies in terms of voting population, numbering 29,419. In the 2000 elections, ten contestants vied for the coveted seat in the Assembly. A look at the profile of the constituency, taking the election results since 1974, would suggest that it was in the grip of neither a single candidate nor a particular party.

Table 6.5

Voting trend in 21 Naoriya Pakhanglakpa constituency since 1974

Year	*Votes polled by the winner*	*Votes polled by nearest rival*	*Difference*
1974	Tokpam Sanajao 3626 (MRP) 32.33%	Wahengbam Angou Singh 3082 (Congress) 27.48%	544
1980	Wahengbam Angou Singh 5320(Congress-U) 38.59%	Akoijam Ibobi 4180 (MPP) 30.32%	1140

(Contd...)

Year	*Votes polled by the winner*	*Votes polled by nearest rival*	*Difference*
1984	Wahengbam Angou Singh 5033 (Congress) 31.48%	Akoijam Ibobi 4130 (MRP) 25.83%	903
1990	Poll could take place, by poll result not available		
1995	A.K. Lanngam 6711 (IND) 32.62%	Wahengbam. Angou Singh 5916 (Congress) 28.76%	795
2000	Wahengbum Leima Devi 5418 (IND) 25.22%	Akoijam Ibobi 3716 (SAP) 17.30	1702
2002	Wahengbam Leima Devi 5712 (Congress) 24.52%	R.K. Anand 4990 (DRPP) 21.42	722
2007	R.K. Anand 10598 (MPP) 39.67%	Keisham Rajen Kumar Singh 7861 (RJD) 29.43	2737

Source: Election Commission of India

After getting elected to the Assembly as an Independent candidate, Wahengbam Leima Devi joined the Congress and fought the 2002 election. She retained the seat with a slender increase in the number of votes polled in her favour but with a slightly lesser percentage. She became a minister in 2002, holding the portfolio of Information and Public Relations and Loktak Authority. She was defeated by R.K. Anand, her long time rival, in 2007. She secured the third position with 6561votes which was, however, more than that votes she had polled in 2002.

The defeat of the sole sitting woman member in the Assembly in an atmosphere of the Congress wave was intriguing. It was alleged that a section of the Congress leadership wanted her defeat, and therefore, actively acted against her by forging an underhand deal with R.K. Anand, a comparatively new face in the election politics in Manipur. An advocate by profession, Anand has been active in various organizations including the DRPP. At any rate, politics of all possibilities worked against her.

(3) **30 Lilong** is known to be a Muslim majority constituency (approximately 79.89%) with an electorate around 26,317. The Meiteis constitute around 19.29 per cent. The Manipuri Muslims are known as 'Pangals'. The Meitei Pangal is known as a cross-breed of Meitei women and Bengali Muslims. The first migration of Bengali Muslims took place during the reign of King Khagemba (1597-1652AD). Their succeeding generations fully assimilated to the Meitei society.[3] Their demographic strength in the constituency would be around 80 per cent.

Lilong constituency is at the outskirts of greater Imphal. It has been always returning a Muslim MLA only since 1974. A profile of the voting trend in the constituency might give a proper insight to religious and ethnic dynamics in the state.

In 1972, when the first Assembly elections were held after Manipur was elevated to the status of a full-fledged state, Lilong's constituency number was 31. It was changed to 30 in 1974. It is an important constituency, once held by held by Alimuddin of the MPP who had been the Chief Minister of the state from March 23, 1972 to July 1974. It was more or less known to be a stronghold of the Congress, for, its candidate had been elected for four times and on four occasions its candidates secured the second position. In 2007 Helaluddin Khan, who contested with a RJD ticket, defeated the sitting Congress MLA Dr. Maniruddin Shaikh. Helaluddin himself was a Congress MLA for three times before he was denied the ticket in 2000. In 1980 he was elected for the first time with the Congress ticket. In the next election held in 1984, he was defeated by the MPP candidate Allauddin by a slender margin of 328 votes. But he returned to the Assembly once again in 1990 with the Congress ticket and retained his seat in 1995. In 2000, he was denied the party ticket to accommodate a new face Dr Maniruddin Shaikh. There was split in the Congress support base leading to the victory of the NCP candidate Allauddin and naturally to the defeat of the Congress candidate and its rebel, who contested with the MSCP ticket. Maniruddin turned the table to his advantage in 2002 but failed to retain the hold on the seat in 2007. Helaluddin's victory by a margin of 1565 votes in 2007 was striking in view of the Congress wave. What then went wrong with the calculations in the Congress? The move to rest the sitting Congress MLA in 2000 in favour of a new face Maniruddin Shaikh went against its fortune. It is believed that Maniruddin was close to the MPCC leadership, more particularly to Okram Ibobi Singh, for which he could manage to snatch the Congress ticket from Helaluddin in 2002. In that election Allauddin, a known face in the constituency was elected. But in the next election held in 2002, Maniruddin Shaikh could unseat Allauddin and enter the Assembly for the first time. It was alleged that Maniruddin became complacent after winning the election in 2002 by a record margin of 3495, votes and distanced himself from his constituency. A number of women groups complained that they expected that he, being a doctor by profession, would redeem his election promise to improve the conditions of the local public health center; but he did not take any steps to improve the much-needed health care establishments as also the public distribution system and the public communication infrastructure. All these infuriated them to campaign vigorously against him and return Helaluddin once again to the Assembly. As a three time MLA, Helaluddin had created a base, which appeared to be solid all through; he was known for his association with the Congress even after he changed his party affiliation. At any rate, Lilong was more or less a Congress bastion. The regional parties like the MPP made a dent in the constituency in the early 1970s, which, however, got eroded by 1980.

Table 6.6
Voting trend in 30 Lilong constituency since 1974

Year	*Votes polled by the winner*	Votes polled by nearest rival	Difference
1974	Alimuddin 5989 (MRP) 59.30%	Abdul Kadir Shah 4111 (Congress) 40.70	1878
1980	Helaluddin Khan 7629 (Congress) 61.43%	Alimuddin 4680 (JP) 26.43%	2949
1984	Alauddin 4369(MRP) 29.01%	Helaluddin Khan 4041 (Congress) 26.83%	328
1990	Helaluddin Khan 8814 (Congress)54.94%	Alauddin 7178 (MPP) 44.74%	1636
1995	Helaluddin Khan 6371 (Congress) 37.73%	Alauddin 5369 (MPP) 31.79%	1002

(Contd...)

Year	*Votes polled by the winner*	Votes polled by nearest rival	Difference
2000	Alauddin 6706 (NCP) 36.56%	Dr. Maniruddin Shaikh 6553 (Congress) 35.72%	153
2002	Dr. Maniruddin Shaikh 9561 (Congress) 39.17%	Helaluddin Khan 6066 (MNC) 31.43	3495
2007	Helaluddin Khan 9848 (RJD) 41.36%	Dr. Maniruddin Shaikh 8283 (Congress) 34.72	1565

Source: Election Commission of India

(4) **31 Thoubal** constituency shot into prominence in 2007 when the Chief Minister decided to contest from it despite the fact that it was not a safe seat for the Congress (Table 6.7). It is known to be a non-Congress seat, most of the time was held by the regional parties. Taking a high risk, Ibobi Singh contested and unseated the sitting three times MLA, Leitanthem Tomba Singh by a huge margin of 6316 votes. Despite the fact that Tomba Singh could increase his tally compared to the last elections by 814 votes, he failed to approach to the figure secured by Ibobi Singh. There were a number of reasons for this. In 2002, it was a five-cornered keen contest in which the difference in votes shared by four other contestants was slender. This time in 2007, it was three-cornered contest in which major players like the MPP, the NCP and the MSCP, who had contested in the previous elections, stayed away from the fray against a heavyweight whose prospect for victory had been pronounced and reassuring. The contest was between the Chief Minister and the sitting MLA. The only Independent contestant, who polled 162 votes, was nowhere. It appeared that while Tomba Singh could retain his support base, he failed to attract the voters

having affiliation to other parties. These votes went to Ibobi Singh for the singular most important reason that he was the Chief Minister of the state. Ibobi's decision to contest from the unsafe constituency was to demolish the putative impression that Thoubal was and would remain an anti-Congress bastion.

Table 6.7
Voting trend in 31 Thoubal constituency since 1974

Year	*Votes polled by the winner*	*Votes polled by nearest rival*	*Difference*
1974	Koijam Mangi Singh 3366 (MRP) 29.90%	Thoudam Krishna Singh 3157 (IND) 28.04%	209
1980	Thoudam Krishna Singh 3701 (MPP) 26.92%	Akoijam Ibomcha 3633 (Congress U) 26.43%	68
1984	Leitanthem Tomba Singh 5316 (JP) 33.83%	Thoudam Krishna Singh 4050 (Congress) 25.77%	1266
1990	Thoudam Krishna Singh 9956 (JD) 51.54%	Leitanthem Tomba Singh 9361 (Congress) 48.46%	595
1995	Leitanthem Tomba Singh 11239 (MPP) 60.19%	Thoudam Krishna Singh 4860 (Congress) 26.03%	6379
2000	Leitanthem Tomba Singh 7527 (MSCP) 37.64%	Abdul Rouf (Temba) 4768 (MPP) 23.84	2759
2002	Leitanthem Tomba Singh 5502 (FMP) 26.45%	T. Mukesh Singh 4777 (Congress) 22.96%	750
2007	Okran Ibobi Singh 17260 (Congress) 72.86%	Leitanthem Tomba Singh 6316 (MPP) 26.68%	6316

Source: Election Commission of India

(5) **34 Wangjing Tentha** appears to be another important constituency for several reasons. It is a traditionally a left dominated area, where the CPI used to return its candidate to the Assembly. In the 2002 elections Dr. Moirangthem Nara Singh was elected with 9247 (43.77%) votes, the margin being 1527 over his Congress adversary, Moirangthem Hemanta Singh. Nara Singh is a theatre personality and has been with the IPTA movement for more than three decades. This time in 2007, he was unexpectedly defeated by his old-time rival. Despite the fact that he improved his support base by securing 10375 votes in absolute figure, in terms of percentage, there was a fall of 1.49%, which proved to be costly when compared with Hemanta Singh's improvement from 36.54 to 44.85 percent (Table 6.8).

Table 6.8
Voting trend in 34 Wangjin Tentha constituency since 1974

Year	*Votes polled by the winner*	*Votes polled by nearest rival*	*Difference*
1974	Saqam Ibomcha Singh IND (2362) 22.41%	Naorem Kunjababu Singh MRP (1982) 18.81%	380
1980	Laishram Saratchandra Singh IND (3221) 25.77%	Moirangthem Nara Singh CPI (2432) 19.46%	789
1984	Moirangthem Nara Singh CPI (3079) 20.06%	Sepem Ibomcha IND (2599) 16.94%	480
1990	Moirangthem Nara Singh CPI (6076) 31.59%	Moirangthm Hemanta Singh Congress (5409) 28.11	667

(Contd...)

Year	*Votes polled by the winner*	*Votes polled by nearest rival*	*Difference*
1995	Moirangthem Hemanta Singh Congress (7638) 41.97%	Moirangthem Nara Singh CPI (5925) 32.55%	1713
2000	Moirangthem Hemanta Singh MSCP (7288) 35.14%	Moirangthem Nara Singh CPI (6703) 32.32%	585
2002	Moirangthem Nara Singh CPI (9247) 43.77%	Moiranthem Hemanta Singh Congress (7720) 36.54%	1527
2007	Moirangthem Hemanta Singh, Congress (11007) 44.85%	Moirangthem Nara Singh, CPI (10328) 42.28%	679

Source: Election Commission of India

The constituency has had a strong base for Moiranthem Nara Singh because of which he could win the election for three times that included two consecutive stints in the Assembly. The Congress, too, had an almost equally strong foundation, for which its candidate Moirangthem Hemanta Singh was elected thrice, including two consecutive terms as in case of Nara Singh. To defeat Nara Singh was not an easy task, considering his association with the cultural life in the state and his decisive win in 2002 election by a margin of 1527 votes. We had a long interview with Nara Singh on April 16, 2007. According to him, it is easy to 'manage' most of the constituencies in Manipur, in view of the smallness of their population size, including his own constituency with mere 12143 voters. He said: "If a contestant spends Rs. 10 million and purchase 9000 voters, it is easy for him to win. And to spend that amount is not a great deal for many aspirants in the state. In this election money power played a decisive role. My rival used that power. I am just helpless in such a situation. An ordinary voter with Rs.1000 in his pocket put by a candidate will be guided by the force of money and not by his conscience." It is difficult to find out the truth in such a statement for want of hard evidence. But the general impression as had been created by the media and also testified to by leading personalities whom we had interviewed, leave enough scope to suspect that money had a role to play in the last Assembly elections in Manipur.

(6) **35 Khangabok** has been known as Ibobi's constituency for a long time. He held this constituency for two consecutive terms from 1984 to 1995 when he had to concede defeat to Laisram Jatra Singh with a considerably big margin of 1147 votes (Table 6.9). He tried to stage a come back in 2000 but had his dream shattered by a thin margin of 52 votes. Eventually he did it in 2002, when he snatched the seat from his long time rival Laisram Jatra Singh by a huge margin of 2330 votes. Soon after the election, as stated already in Chapter III, he became the Chief Minister in a coalition arrangement. Thus, this constituency came to be known as Chief Minister's constituency. Ibobi Singh, as already stated, also contested from 31 Thoubal constituency, which was traditionally a non-Congress one. However, Khangabok was a safe constituency for him, despite the fact that his arch rival made an anti-incumbency campaign focusing on where the Chief Minister had failed to redeem his promises. The MPP too could muster support from other regional parties to rally behind a common plank to defeat the Chief Minister.

Consequently, it became virtually a direct contest between Okram Ibobi Singh and Laishram Jatra Singh, with the third candidate Haji Asrab of the SP, virtually a non-entity. Remaining out of focus, Haji Asrab could secure only 180 votes, and therefore, had to forfeit his deposit. There was heavy poll, 91.53 per cent, due mainly to the vigorous campaign by both the main contenders. While the Chief Minister could improve his tally, both in absolute figures and in terms of percentage, the combined opposition under the banner of the MPP could hardly have any significant impact. The results show that Laishram Jatra Singh got fewer votes than earlier, with the percentage of votes polled by him slumping down from 43.87 to 36.34. It was not unexpected; as the Chief Minister of the state, Ibobi Singh had more or less an unblemished record of clean image and functional disposition, which could not be demolished easily. The difference in the margin of votes secured by Ibobi Singh, 6918 in a straight contest and the percentage of votes polled (62.98) indicate, in unmistakable terms, the magnitude of his popularity in the constituency.

Table 6.9
Voting trend in 35 Khangabok constituency since 1974

Year	*Votes polled by the winner*	*Votes polled by nearest rival*	*Difference*
1974	Thokehom Achouba CPI (3491) 33.43%	Moirangthem Borajao Singh MRP (2820) 27.00%	671
1980	Thokehom Achouba CPI (3139) 24.93%	Abdul Jabar IND (2812) 22.34%	327
1984	Okram Ibobi Singh IND (4157) 25.21%	Moirangthem Borajao Singh IND (3303) 20.59%	854

(Contd...)

Year	*Votes polled by the winner*	*Votes polled by nearest rival*	*Difference*
1990	Okram Ibobi Singh Congress (7320) 35.21%	Moirangthem Borajao MPP (4998) 24.04%	2322
1995	Laishram Jatra Singh MPP (8021) 39.99%	Okram Ibobi Singh Congress (6884) 34.32%	1147
2000	Laishram Jatra Singh MPP (11144) 48.73%	Okram Ibobi Singh Congress (11092) 48.50%	52
2002	Okram Ibobi Singh Congress (12897) 53.54%	Laishram Jatra Singh FMP (10567) 43.87%	2330
2007	Okram Ibobi Singh Congress (16782) 62.98%	Laishram Jatra Singh MPP (9864) 36.34%	6918

Source: Election Commission of India

(7) **36 Wabgai** is a test case to show how division of votes in the same political bastion could lead to the victory of a comparatively lesser known candidate. This constituency had been a ground for stiff competition between two individuals – Abdul Salam and Mayengbam Manihar Singh, since 1990. Salam was not a new face in the fray; he won the seat in 1980 as an Independent candidate, Manihar Singh wrested the seat in 1984, pushing the sitting MLA to the third position. Table 6.10 reveals that the both Salam and Manihar Singh used to change party affiliation quite frequently. Salam started off as an Independent, and went to the fold of the MPP and then to the Congress. His rival Mayengbam Singh did not lag behind. He too changed his party at least thrice. In the election of 2000, he won with a Congress ticket, but was denied the party ticket two years later, forcing him to take shelter in the MSCP, which, as stated

earlier, was a splinter outfit of the Congress, and had to face defeat at the hands of Abdul Salam, who returned to the Congress fold just before the election. In 2007, there was a split of the Congress votes among the Congress, the MSCP and the NCP, all originally belonging to the same stock. The combined votes could be much higher than the winner's. The three-way split in the Congress support base helped a new comer in politics, Usham Deben Singh of the CPI, to steal the show and get elected to the Assembly with a slender margin. It was argued that the NCP, which stayed away from the contest in 2002, ate away much of the Congress cake.

Table 6.10
Voting trend in 36 Wabgai constituency

Year	*Votes polled by the winner*	*Votes polled by nearest rival*	*Difference*
1974	Habibur Rahman Congress (4271) 43.29%	Naorem Mohandas MRP (2996) 30.37%	1276
1980	Abdul Salam IND (2634) 21.48%	Naorem Mohandas IND (1894) 15.44%	740
1984	Mayengbam Manihar Singh IND (3046) 20.82%	Naorem Mohandas IND (2954) 20.19%	92
1990	Mayengbam Manihar Singh Congress (4757) 27.78%	Abdul Salam MPP (4553) 26.59%	209
1995	Abdul Salam MPP (6766) 38.21%	Mayengnam Manihar Singh Congress (4861) 27.45%	1905
2000	Mayengnam Manihar Singh Congress (6282) 32.61%	Abdul Salam MPP (4066) 21.11%	2216

(Contd...)

Year	*Votes polled by the winner*	*Votes polled by nearest rival*	*Difference*
2002	Abdul Salam Congress (7512) 38.17%	Mayengbam Manihar Singh MSCP (7496) 38.09%	16
2007	Dr. Usham Deben Singh CPI (6725) 30.95%	Mayengbam Manihar Singh MSCP (6664) 30.60%	61

Source: Election Commission of India

(8) **41 Chandel** constituency is essentially a tribal one, where the Kukis have a substantial presence in the border areas adjacent to Myanmar. The ethnic Maring community, which is a sub-tribe of the Nagas, has also sizeable population in this constituency. They are estimated to be the largest one in Tengnoupal, which is adjacent to Chandel. The UNC supported candidate, L. Benjamin, appeared to be confident of his victory. It was one of the constituencies which experienced very high voter turnouts in the state to the tune of 94.01 per cent. It has also a sizeable Mizo population also, because of which H.T. Thungam could capture the seat twice (1974 and 1984). This is known as an essentially non-Congress constituency, where no Congress candidate could win till now. There was a tough fight in 1990 offered by H.T. Thungan as a Congress candidate against the JD candidate but was defeated by a slender margin of 20 votes. To put it precisely, Chandel had always been a non-Congress, Naga dominated constituency where other national parties such as the BJP and the RJD could, however, make a mark. In 2002, the BJP candidate B.D. Behring Anal convincingly defeated the MSCP candidate by an unprecedented huge margin of 14,469 votes, the highest so far, proving thereby that the nationalist fervour in the constituency had been rising. The 2007

election reinforced that impression, when the RJD candidate secured 17,424 votes (44.17%) to put the nearest rival, an Independent candidate, in total disarray. It is interesting to note that the UNC's call not to field candidates of national parties had a mixed response, while the RJD stole the show, others including the Congress and the BJP, did not field any candidate openly but backed some of the five Independent candidates. It could be attributed to the fear psychosis created by the UNC diktat. The fact that the UNC supported Independent candidate could manage to secure only 19.17 per cent of the votes clearly bears out that the claim of the secessionist forces to having a base in this constituency is undounded. This happened in other constituencies too which will be focused in a relevant section. The most striking feature is that in this Naga dominated constituency a Kuki candidate won the seat defeating the UNC sponsored candidate by a huge margin of 9861 votes. It is a clear indication as to what extent the issue of Nagalim remained a decisive one in the Naga psyche.

Table 6.11
Voting trend in 41 Chandel constituency

Year	*Votes polled by the winner*	*Votes polled by nearest rival*	*Difference*
1974	H.T. Thungam MHU (3490) 24.45%	Nula Thumsing Congress (3303) 24.44%	187
1980	Satkholal KNA (6075) 33.81%	L.H. Angno Congress (3251) 18.10%	2824
1984	H.T. Thungam IND (4535) 22.04%	Paokhhang ICS (3874) 18.83%	661

(Contd...)

Year	*Votes polled by the winner*	*Votes polled by nearest rival*	*Difference*
1990	B.D. Behring Anal JD (6653)25.41%	H.T. Thungam Congress (6633) 25.33%	20
1995	Hangkhanpao JD (13030)45.43%	L. Benjamin FPM (10464) 36.48%	2566
2000	Hangkhanpao RJD (13187) 39.28%	B.D. Behring Anal MSCP(11333) 19.18%	1854
2002	B.D. Behring Anal BJP (23219) 64.71%	T. Chaungsihaokip MSCP (8750) 24.39%	14469
2007	Thangkholun Haokip RJD (17424) 44.17%	L. Benjamin IND (7563) 19.17%	9861

Source: Election Commission of India

(9) **48 Mao** constituency is one of the Naga inhabited areas in which the UNC had strong hold, and therefore, none except the Congress could defy the UNC command. In the five-cornered contest, all others, including the UNC candidate M. Thohrii joined the battle as Independents. M. Thohrii, who had contested as a SAP candidate in 2002 and had secured the third position, (10628 votes i.e. 24.28 per cent votes) won the 2007 election, with a comfortable margin (Table 6.12). The sitting Congress MLA, R.K. Thekho was relegated to the last position. He secured 188 votes and lost his deposit. The improvement in the tally made by Thohrii by 5893 was indeed remarkable. The Congress votes went to him for which R.K. Thekho had to cut a sorry figure in 2007. The figures displayed in Table 6.11 suggest a lot.

Table 6.12
Voting trend in 48 Mao constituency

Year	*Votes polled by the winner*	*Votes polled by nearest rival*	*Difference*
1974	R.K. Thekho MHU (3764) 26.76%	Soso Lorho Congress (3612) 25.68%	152
1980	Soso Lorho Congress (6897) 36.09%	R.K. Thekho JP (5576) 29.18%	1321
1984	S. Lorho Congress (7841) 34.03%	Puni Beso IND (7705) 33.44%	138
1990	S. Lorho Congress (10425) 32.87%	M. Thohrii ICS(SCS) (9576) 30.19%	849
1995	M. Thohrii ICS (22310) 62.95%	S. Lorho Congress (13108) 36.99%	9202
2000	M. Thohrii Congress (23149) 58.85%	S. Lorho MSCP (13813) 35.12%	9336
2002	R.K. Thekho Congress (13387) 30.58%	Soso Lorho FMP (12936) 29.55%	451
2007	M. Thohrii IND (16521) 41.81%	Woba Joram IND (11000) 27.84%	5521

Source: Eiection Commission of India

Three contestants – R.K. Thekho, Soso Lorho and M. Thohrii – happen to be the key players in the constituency. But none of them could retain their seats in the next election. All of them have changed their party affiliations, virtually a normal feature in the state. However, in 2007 they had to contest as Independent candidates, fearing the wrath of the militants. M. Thohrii has a long association with the Congress, despite the fact that he had ditched his party to join breakaway factions, twice in his political career. This time, he secured the support of the UNC and could come out victorious, defeating another Independent by a huge margin of 5521 votes. This is one of five seats that the UNC supported Independent candidates captured.

(10) **51 Saitu** is an important Kuki dominated constituency, which was held by the Congress MLA Ngamthang Haokip. He captured the seat defeating Haokholet Kipgen, a SAP candidate, in the 2002 elections by a considerably large margin (Table 6.13). In 2007 Haokholet Kipgen contested the election as an Independent candidate reportedly to win the support of the UNC. This arrangement enabled Kipgen to improve his fortune substantially from 8359 votes in 2002 to 17637, and thus, to defeat the Congress candidate in a convincing way. It is important to note that Haokip improved his voting tally both in absolute figure (4257) and in terms of percentage (1.59) over his past record in 2002, but it was insufficient to win the election owing to high turnout in favour of his Independent UNC supported rival, who polled a record number of votes. Let us have a look at the voting trend in the constituency.

Table 6.13
Voting trend in 51 Saitu constituency

Year	*Votes polled by the winner*	*Votes polled by nearest rival*	*Difference*
1974	Zampu KNA (2458) 20.84%	Paokhosei Congress (2446) 20.74%	12
1980	L.S. John IND (2615) 18.54%	Althing Lhingjaneng JP (2496) 17.70%	119

(Contd...)

Year	*Votes polled by the winner*	*Votes polled by nearest rival*	*Difference*
1984	S.L. Paokhosei Congress (5146) 26.89%	Jampao Haokip IND (2974) 15.54%	2172
1990	Ngamthang Haokip MPP (8468) 40.60%	S.L. Paokhosei Congress (6829) 32.74%	1639
1995	Ngamthang Haokip MPP (9680) 38.53%	Alar Thoitak IND (7303) 29.07%	2377
2000	Haokholet Kipgen FPM (14580) 48.24%	Ngamthang Haokip MSCP (14394) 47.63%	183
2002	Ngamthang Haokip Congress (9893) 41.56%	Haokholet Kipgen SAP (8357) 26.53%	1538
2007	Haokholet Kipgen IND (17637) 53.79%	Ngamthang Haokip Congress (14150) 43.15%	3487

Source: Election Commission of India

It is evident from Table 6.13 that the 51 Saitu constituency had been a ground for keen contest between Ngamthang Haokip and Haokholet Kipgen, both belong to same Kuki tribe, for the last seven years and in the three Assembly elections. Both of them changed their party affiliations. The sitting MLA Ngamthan Haokip's loss to Haokholet Kipgen with a huge margin was not unexpected. Despite the fact that Ngamthang Haokip improved his support base to a considerable extent, Haokholet Kipgen's improvement was too formidable to deny him obvious victory.

(11) **53 Tamenglong,** a Naga dominated area, presented a fascinating case of people's protest against

violence and kidnapping, indulged in by insurgent elements. Most of the Nagas of this area belong to Zeliangrong Kabui community. Khangthuanang Panmei, who had contested the 2002 election as a Congress candidate and secured the second position with 40.60 per cent votes (Table 6.14), reportedly was reluctant to take the risk of contesting the election with a national party ticket in view of the threat issued by the UNC. So in 2007, he decided to contest as an Independent. An insurgent group kidnapped him soon after he had filed his nomination papers. His supporters spearheaded the election campaign on his behalf, and eventually brought victory to him. It was a rare testimony of courage and determination to frustrate the attempted hijacking of a free poll by insurgents. Table 6.12 shows that in the five-cornered battle, the kidnapped candidate secured 41.35 per cent votes, much ahead of his nearest rival.

Table 6.14
Voting trend in 53 Tamenglong constituency

Year	*Votes polled by the winner*	*Votes polled by nearest rival*	*Difference*
1974	T.P. Kiulengpou MHU (3152) 43.20%	K. Huriang IND (1602) 21.96%	1550
1980	K. Huriang IND (3318) 36.05%	Phenrong JP (2043) 22.19%	1275
1984	Jangamlung Panmei Congress (5035) 44.16%	Ningthan Panmei IND (2420) 21.23%	2615
1990	Daisin Pamei JD (5024) 32.95%	G. Phenrong Congress (3797) 24.90%	1227

(Contd...)

Year	*Votes polled by the winner*	*Votes polled by nearest rival*	*Difference*
1995	Samuel Jendai SAP (6515) 41.29%	Daisin Panmei Congress (6029) 38.21%	486
2000	Samuel Jendai MSCP (7572)44.49%	Khangthuanang Panmei SAP (4361) 25.61%	3211
2002	Samuel Jendai FMP (9696) 53.91%	Khangthuanang Panmei Congress (7302) 40.60%	2394
2007	Khangthuanang Panmei IND (8460) 41.35%	Samuel Jendai IND (6217) 30.25%	2281

Source: Election Commission of India

Just as Panmei, despite his earlier Congress affiliation, contested as an Independent, Samuel Jendai too contested as an Independent candidate. It was not easy to defeat Samuel Jendai, a sitting MLA for three consecutive terms. He had defeated Panmei twice before, with considerably huge margins. But the kidnapping episode engineered a significant sympathy vote to enhance Panmei's poll fortune by 1156 over his last tally. It could not be ascertained, due to lack of credible evidence, as to who was behind the kidnapping. However, it is commonly believed that the insurgent group working for the UNC supported candidate Samuel Jendai was responsible for kidnapping Panmei in a bid to ensure easy victory.

It is interesting to find that in a constituency like **54 Nungba**, Gangmumei Kamei (Independent), a two times MLA (1995-2000 and 2000-2002), who reportedly sought and secured the blessings of the NSCN (IM)[4], lost the election to the sitting Congress candidate, Gaikhangam, by a margin of 5,583 votes. In a four-cornered battle Kamei polled only 33.10 per cent votes (6012 votes), while the winning Congress candidate secured 11,595 (63.85%) votes, which is much higher compared to his own previous record of securing 6977 votes. It is noteworthy that Kamei was a Professor of History at the Manipur University and was one of the founder members of the Federal Party of Manipur. It appeared that despite his best efforts he could not enlist the support and sympathy of the UNC, which remained non-committal, because of the absence of the consent of the NSCN (IM). It was indeed difficult for him to win against Gaikhangam who had been working for his constituency for the last six years as an MLA and remaining in touch with the electorate since 1984.

Another interesting case was the election of Thounaojam Shyamkumar of MPP who contested from 7 Andro constituency. He was arrested in New Delhi at Indira Gandhi International Airport on October 2, 2006 along with two UNLF cadres on charge of having links with the said underground outfit and was put in jail. His supporters took the responsibility of the campaign and eventually secured 18,388 votes. His rival Salam Chandra Singh of the Congress, a sitting MLA holding the constituency since 1995 secured only 5157 in this five cornered fight. This is a clear demonstration of people's support for a candidate who was allegedly detained on a "cooked up charge". Shyamkumar had been contesting from this constituency since 2000 at first with a NCP ticket and then with a Congress ticket in 2002; each time fortune did not smile on him. He was later on released on March 21, 2007 after he won the election with a thumping margin.[5]

The UNC managed to win in five constituencies – 43 Phungyar, 44 Ukhrul, 45 Chingai, 48 Mao and 52 Tamei- out of eleven where it fielded its candidates in the Naga dominated areas. Some of its stalwarts, like Samuel Jendai and S. Kho John had to taste defeat, with significant margins. It reinforces the doubt as to what extent the Nagas themselves are politically and emotionally attached to the demand for Nagalim. There was heavy polling in all the 11 constituencies (Table 6.13). The heavy turnout is a clear indication that electorate participation in each constituency was indeed very high.

Table 6.15
Turnout in UNC dominated constituencies

Sl. No	*Name of the constituencies*	*% of turnout*	*Winner*
1	42 Tengnoupal	93.81	W. Morung Haokip, (IND)
2	43 Phungyar	82.27	K. Wungnaoshang (IND)
3	44 Ukhrul	73.10	Danny Shaiza (IND)
4	45 Chingai	77.50	Dr. Khashim Ruiyah (IND)
5	46 Saikul	85.53	Doukhomang Khogsai (NCP)
6	48 Mao	80.34	M. Thohrii (IND)
7	49 Tadubi	94.77	K. Raina (IND)
8	51 Saitu	84.57	Haokholet Kipgen (IND)
9	52 Tamei	80.65	Awangbow Newmei (IND)
10	53Tamenglong	80.83	Khangthuanang Panmei (IND)
11	54 Nungba	86.08	Gaikhangam (Congress)

Source: Election Commission of India

The UNC's call to the electorate to boycott the national parties appears to have gone against its candidates. Not only a few national parties like the Congress and the RJD fought the elections and won seats, but the common electorate also refused to obey the diktat. That is why 6 non-UNC candidates could win, pushing the militant backed Independents to the second position in the winners list of eleven. The racial and territorial homogeneity of the people living in the Naga inhabited areas did not work in favour of the UNC, thereby proving a point that the purported electoral arithmetic is speculative only.

REFERENCES

1. Coaliton politics started emerging soon after the 1967 general elections. The trend which was going to dominate in Indian politics has been eloquently tapped in a highly analytical article of Paul R. Brass, "Coalition Politics in North India", *American Political Science Review*, Vol. 62, No. 4, December 1968, pp 1174-1191. For some understanding of coalition politics in India in the recent years see Mahendra Prasad Singh and Anil Mishra (eds), *Coalition Politics in India: Problems and Prospects* (New Delhi: Manohar, 2004); Bidyut Chakrabarty, *Forging Power: Coaltion Politics in India* (New Delhi: Oxford University Press, 2006)
2. Gangmumei Kamei was a candidate of the FPM who contested under the banner of the MPP from the Nungba (ST) constituency and was defeated by his Congress rival Gaikhangam by 5583 votes. A former professor of History in Manipur University, he is one of the founder members of the party. He was interviewed at his residence on April 16, 2007.
3. United Committee of Manipur, *Influx of Migrants into Manipur: A Threat to the Indigenous Ethnic People* (Imphal: UMC, 2000) p.18.

4. Gangmumai Kamei, a Tankhul Naga, decided to contest as an Independent, reportedly, to enlist the support of the UNC as well as the NSCN (IM), a step which did not yield anything favourable for him.
5. *Poknapham*, March 22, 2007.

7

CONCLUSION

Politics in India has become more and more an election centric game. Everything that relates to power tends to rotate around the prospects of electoral gain. It is mainly because of the fact that political legitimacy in wielding power is drawn from elections held at various levels, - local, state and national. In a federal structure like that of India's, despite the unitary character of the Indian state, the federating states enjoy enormous powers. Even at the local levels, there has been substantial devolution of power, ushered in by the 73rd and 74th amendments to the Indian Constitution. Naturally, all elections have captured the center stage of political process in the country as indicators of future accommodation of interests, arrangements and adjustments contemplated by political actors and participants.

Just as all state elections are important, the Assembly elections held in Manipur in 2007 was indeed thrilling and epoch-making for several reasons as already spelt out in relevant sections of the preceding Chapters. To recapitulate, 2007 elections had taken place at the end of the tenure of a stable government, which was illusive since 1967. Second, the UNC's call to boycott all national parties was a serious challenge to free and fair elections. It appeared that the national parties would not be able to contest and campaign in the 11 Naga inhabitant constituencies, for the UNC's call had the backing of the NSCN (IM). Third, all the regional parties assembled under the banner of the MPP, forgetting their party identities in order to put up a formidable challenge to the national parties, more particularly the Congress. It was for the first time that such a rally of regional sentiment could be seen in the electoral politics in Manipur. Fourth, there had been an unparalleled show of strength on the flag day organized by the Congress, giving a clear message to the electorate as to its resources in terms of manpower, infrastructure and finance. It was followed by the visit of Manmohan Singh, the Prime Minister of India, to campaign for the party, and two unprecedented visits by the Congress President, Sonia Gandhi. The Opposition parties failed to match these royal exercises. It indicated the trend of the electioneering.

Despite the fact that Manipur had been reeling under the spate of a prolonged and endemic insurgency related crises, which had robbed the basics of a normal civic life, the popular response to the elections had always been encouraging. The fact that since 1974 when the insurgency situation in Manipur was at the peak and violence of grave magnitude had been the order of the day, the electorate turned out to exercise their right of franchise in a massive way (Table 3.15). It is a clear indication of commoners' allegiance to the Constitution of the country. As in the earlier occasions, more recently in 2004, at the time of Lok Sabha elections, a number of militant outfits called for a boycott. Ignoring such a call,

64 per cent of the electorate came out to cast their votes. These are the hard evidence to argue that for the common citizen to exercise the right to franchise is a birth right, which could not be taken away by the power of guns.

Three issues – the AFSPA, the Nagalim and the development of the economy of the state, captured the attention of all the political parties, as detailed in the relevant Chapter. As the electioneering reached the peak, the development issues gathered momentum and overshadowed the other two. The UPA Chairperson, Sonia Gandhi, while addressing a public rally during her first visit, mentioned that the AFSPA could be withdrawn on an experimental basis in the Imphal valley. But she refrained from making any statement on the issue in her second campaign visit. The Prime Minister paid attention to the task of development only and took the credit for revitalization of the economy and academic environment, including the elevation of the Manipur University to the status of a central university. While the Nagalim issue, articulated in the language of integration of the Naga inhabited areas, drew attention in a few constituencies, it failed to make a mark in Manipur as a whole. To state precisely, the issues of development, so intrinsically associated with the political stability in the state, sidelined the other two politically charged issues. The issue of integration of Naga inhabited areas is anathema to the Maities' commitment to the protection of the territorial integrity of Manipur.

Going by the argument advanced by a few leading political practitioners in Manipur, two issues were placed before the electorate as a referendum – the withdrawal of the AFSPA and the integration of the Naga inhabited areas under the ambit of 'Nagalim'. The regional sentiment, as expressed under the umbrella organization called the MPP was in favour of the withdrawal of the AFSPA. Most of the Meitei civil society organizations appeared to have backed the election plank of the MPP. The local media too extended support by focusing on the need to withdraw this draconian security arrangement. The fact that MPP could secure only 5 seats reveals the kind of support the party could muster in favour of its cause and the political plank. It is argued that 'money power' played a role. If that is the argument for the defeat of the most of the MPP candidates it does not speak well of the support base of the regional forces that sacrificed a cause at the altar of monetary benefit. The referendum seeking a mandate for the withdrawal of the AFSPA was lost. It is interesting to note that the post election political atmosphere in Manipur has not been charged with the said demand. This also leads one to question the hold of the civil society organizations on among the common masses. It is easy to collect thousands of people to stage a demonstration and a long protest march or to impose bandh or curfew. But to win over the voters on the day of election is a different matter, so is to translate that visible demonstration of popular will to a decisive electoral output; for, standing alone, in front of the ballot box, a voter decides what his inner mind tells him to do.

For the UNC the issue of 'integration of Naga dominated areas' was a referendum, though not articulated in unequivocal language, put before the electorate in all the 11 constituencies which were apparently known to be the strongholds of the Naga tribes. The result was a big setback and has undoubtedly weakened its cause. The fact that only 5 out of 11 candidates supported by the UNC could win the elections, implies in unmistakable terms, that this is not the core issue in the hearts of the majority. One has to take note of the massive turnout in all these 11 constituencies, where the polling ranged from 73.10 to 94.77 per cent (Table 4.13). The acts of intimidation, kidnapping and violence did not cow down the voters who did take a decisive action on the polling day.

Issues of development touched the core of the electorate mind. The electorate was firm to sustain the political stability that the state experienced for five years, after a long spell of political crisis. They wanted to strengthen the polity by a decisive mandate in favour of a single party, so that there was to be no repetition of the same crisis. In this endeavour, the electorate rejected the regional sentiment represented by leaders, whose consistency record was too dismal to impress the common masses. Besides, the mandate was expressed in unequivocal terms. The integration of Manipur was a serious matter, put against the backdrop of Naga's claim for integration of Naga inhabited areas, which could not be compromised. The Assembly elections of 2007 was also a decisive referendum favouring territorial integration of Manipur. A hill-vallley divide could be seen in the result. The Meitei dominated valley favoured the Congress while the ST constituencies (18 all total), located mostly in the hill areas, elected non-Congress candidates (Appendix V).

It is interesting to see that no political party could match the Congress in the campaign. The way the ruling party mustered the support of the central leaders is a point to be noted. The visit of the Prime Minister and the two visits of the UPA Chairperson, and the campaign spearheaded by a host of members of the central leadership brought the party to the fore in the victory arena; none else could match this. The fact that no other party could reach even the two digit figure in the victory table indicates the manner in which the voters put the regional sentiment on the back seat of political process in the trouble torn state. It also indicates, in unmistakable terms, that the issues of development registered primacy in the election politics in Manipur.

The popular mandate was decisive for stability and development, and hence much needed change in the political culture of the state.

The 2007 elections provided an opportunity to both the state and the Central Governments to redraw their priorities. While the insurgency related problems would continue to evade a durable solution for reasons of expediency and political compulsions faced by the state and non-state actors, the development issues cannot afford to wait and hence demand immediate attention. The need for an urgent action plan to accelerate the process of economic and human development in the state, is an urgent imperative, which the authoritative decision-makers cannot ignore.

It is argued that position issues which are vital to the electorate matter in elections.[1] That is why political parties and social groups help voters make sense of political issues. Consistent orientation towards issues provides a critical link between voters and the candidates/parties. This is the job of the campaigners. Successful issue-based campaigns propagate strong message to attract the voters to a party or candidate. The voters tend to connect their issue preferences to the party or the candidate. In the case of Manipur, such a directional scenario was developed by the Congress to link issues of development and political stability, making these two sides of the same coin, enabling the voters to find themselves closer to the party and its candidates; thus, it became easier for the party to come back to power with a decisive mandate, which the political pundits could not foresee. In other words, the political situation in the state demanded a stable government. The voters became mature enough to identify the party that could bring a change in the political scenario and provide the much needed stability. One could, therefore, see the pattern in proximity of the issues and the preference of the voters in the critically important 9th Assembly elections in Manipur.

It is interesting to note that the people's verdict did not falter soon after the elections. Immediately after the election, there was vacancy in two seats. Thokchom Nava Kumar Singh of No. 1 Khundrakpam Assembly constituency died soon after the election. He was elected with the NCP ticket. In the by-election his son Thokchom Lokeswar Singh contested with a Congress ticket and won the seat. Chief Minister Okram Ibobi Singh vacated the 35 Khangabok constituency and his wife Okram Landhoni Devi contested the bye-election successfully. The fact that the Congress captured both the seats not only raised its tally in the Assembly, but also enhanced its prestige and confidence. The voters remained consistent in making their choice clear and loud.

It logically demands that the ruling state actors show consistency in the choice and efforts to redeem the promises made before the electorate. The perspective of the state actors needs reorientation. It has to engage in a paradigm shift – from security obsession to development commitment. Looking at the way the people of Manipur played a decisive role in giving their mandate on a number of vitally important issues in a striking manner, it would be wrong to look at this highly resourceful state from the perspective of internal security alone. Taking the cue from the decisive turnout of the voters to decide upon those vital issues, the policy makers need to prioritize the development agenda over the security agenda. The taste of election politics, and of privileges associated democratic set up, are too strong and tempting to fall in favour of militancy.

A state performing the traditional role as a gateway to South East Asian countries, has inevitable and desirable stakes in the era of globalization and in the context of India's currently much discussed 'Look East Policy'. Manipur provides the landing ground of the benefits that are bound to come from the honest implementation of the policy. So many developments including the most visible one in terms of surface connectivity through the Asian Highway are taking place. It will be too costly for the nation if it fails to take note of these positive developments and remains obsessed only with the negative ones. A vibrant nation with boundless vision cannot afford to fail.

REFERENCES

1. Donald E. Stroke, "Spatial models of party competition", *American Political Science Review*, Vol. 57, No. 1, 1963, pp. 368-377.

APPENDIX I

Chief Ministers of Manipur (1963-2007)

Sl. No.	*Name*	*From*	*To*
1.	M.Koireng Singh	01-07-1963	12-01-1967
2.	Koireng Singh	20-03-1967	04-10- 1967
3.	L. Thambou Singh	13-10-1967	25-10-1967
4.	M. Koireng Singh	19-02-1968	16-10-1969
5.	Alimuddin	23-03-1972	28-03-1973
6.	Alimuddin	04-03-1974	08-07-1974
7.	Yangmasho Shaiza	10-07-1974	05-12-1974
8.	R.K. Dorendro Singh	06-12-1974	23-07-1975
9.	R.K. Dorendro Singh	23-07-1975	13-05-1977
10.	Yangmasho Shaiza	29-06-1977	14-11-1979
11.	R.K. Dorendro Singh	14-01-1980	26-11-1980
12.	Rishang Keishing	27-11-1980	28-02-1981
13.	Rishang Keishing	19-06-1981	04-01-1985
14.	Rishang Keishing	04-01-1985	04-03-1988
15.	R.K. Jaichandra	04-03-1988	12-02-1990
16.	R.K. Ranbir Singh	23-02-1990	07-01-1992
17.	R.K. Dorendra Singh	09-04-1992	30-12-1993
18.	Rishang Keishing	14-12-1994	24-02-1995
19.	Rishang Keishing	25-02-1995	15-12-1997
20.	W. Nipamacha Singh	16-12-1997	01-03-2000
21.	W. Nipamacha Singh	02-03-2000	14-02-2001
22.	Radhabinod Koijam	15-02-2001	01-06-2001
23.	Okram Ibobi Singh	07-03-2002	28-02-2007
24.	Okram Ibobi Singh	02-03-2007	Continuing

(Source: *Statistical Abstract Manipur 2005*, Directorate of Economic & Statistics, Government of Manipur)

APPENDIX II

Treaty of Yandaboo: February 24, 1826

Article 1 There shall be perpetual peace and friendship between the Honourable Company on the one part, and His Majesty the King of Ava on the other.

Article 2 His Majesty the King of Ava renounces all claims upon, and will abstain from all future interferences with the principality of Assam and its dependencies, and also with the contiguous petty States of Cachar and Jyntea.

With regard to Munnipore, it is stipulated that, should Gumbheer Singh desire to return to that country, he shall be recognized by the king of Ava as Rajah thereof.

(Signed Archibald Campbell) (L.S.)

Largeen Meonja,
(Woonghee) Signed) T.C.Robertson
Captain Royal Navy (L.S.)
(Seal of the Lotoo) (Signed) Hy.D.Chads
Captain Royal Navy (L.S.)
Shwagum Woon
Atawoon

Source: N.Sanajaoba, *Manipur: Treaties and Documents, (1110-1971)*, 1993, p. 17

APPENDIX III

Manipur Merger Agreement

Agrement Made this twenty-first day of September 1949 between the Governor General of India and His Highness the Maharaja of Manipur.

Whereas in the best interest of the State of Manipur as well as the Dominion of India it is desirable to provide for the administration of the said State by or under the authority of the dominion Government.

IT IS HEREBY AGREED AS FOLLOWS:

ARTICLE I

His Highness the Maharaja of Manipur hereby cedes to the Dominion Government full and exclusive authority, jurisdiction and powers for and in relation to the governance of the State and agrees to transfer the administration of the State to the Dominion Government on the fifteenth day of October 1949 (hereinafter referred to as "the said day").

As from the said day the Dominion Government will be competent to exercise the said powers, authority and jurisdiction in such manner and through such agency as it may think fit.

ARTICLE II

His Highness the Maharaja shall continue to enjoy the same personal rights, privileges, dignities, titles, authority over religious observances, customs, usages, rites and ceremonies and institutions incharge of the same in the State, which he would have enjoyed had this agreement not been made.

ARTICLE III

His Highness the Maharaja shall effect from the said day by entitled to receive for his life-time from the revenues of the State annually for his Privy Purse the sum of Rupees three lakh free of all taxes.

This amount is intended to cover all the expenses of the Ruler and his family, including expenses on account of his personal staff and armed guards, maintenance of his residences, marriages and other ceremonies, etc. and the allowances to the ruler's relations who on the date of execution of this agreement were in receipt of such allowances from the revenues of the State, and will neither be increased nor reduced for any reason whatsoever.

The Government of India undertake that the said sum of Rupees three lakhs shall be paid to His Highness the Maharaja in four equal installments in advance in the beginning of quarter from the State treasury or at such other treasury as may be specified by the Government of India.

ARTICLE IV

His Highness the Maharaja shall be entitled to the full ownership, use and enjoyment of all private properties (as distinct from State properties) belonging to him on the date of this agreement.

His Highness the Maharaja will furnish to the Dominion Government before the first January 1950 an inventory of all the immovable property, securities and cash balance held by him as such private property.

If any dispute arises as to whether any item of property is the private property of His Highness the Maharaja or State property, it shall be referred to a judicial officer qualified to be appointed as a High Court Judge, and the decision of the officer shall be final and binding on both parties.

Provided that His Highness the Maharaja's right to the use of the residences known as " Redlands" and " Les

Chatalettes" in Shillong, and the property in the town of Gauhati known as "Manipuri Basti" shall not be questioned.

ARTICLE V

All the members of His Highness' family shall be entitled to all the personal rights, privileges, dignities and titles enjoyed by them whether within or outside the territories of the State, immediately before the 15th August 1947.

ARTICLE VI

The Dominion Government guarantees the succession, according to law and custom, to the *gaddi* of the state and to His Highness the Maharaja's personal rights, privileges, dignities, titles, authority over religious observances, customs, usages, rites and ceremonies and institutions in charge of the same in the State.

ARTICLE VII

No enquiry shall be made by or under the authority of the Government of India, and no proceedings shall lie in any Court in Manipur, against His Highness the Maharaja, whether in a personal capacity or otherwise, in respect of anything done or omitted to be done by him or under his authority during the period of his administration of that state.

ARTICLE VIII

(1) The Government of India hereby guarantees either the continuance in service of the permanent members of the Public Services of Manipur on conditions which will be not less advantageous than those on which they were serving before the date on which the administration of Manipur is made over to the Government of India or the payment of reasonable compensation.

(2) The Government of India further guarantees the

continuance of pensions and leave salaries sanctioned by His Highness the Maharaja to servants of the State who have retired or proceeded on leave preparatory to retirement, before the date on which the administration of Manipur is added over to the Government of India.

(3) The Government of India also undertake to make suitable provisions for the employment of Manipuris in the various branches of the Public Services, and in every way encourage Manipuris to join them. They also undertake to preserve various laws, customs and conventions prevailing in the State pertaining to the social, economic and religious life of the people.

ARTICLE IX

Except with the previous sanction of the Government of India no proceedings, civil or criminal, shall be instituted against any person in respect of any act done or purporting to be done in the execution of his duties as a servant of the State before the day on which the administration is made over to the Government of India.

In confirmation whereof Mr. Vapal Pangunni Menon, Adviser to the Government of India in the Ministry of States, has appended his signature on behalf and with the authority of the Governor General and His Highness Maharaja Bodh Chandra Singh, Maharaja of Manipur has appended his signature on behalf of himself, his heirs and successors.

Sd/
BODH CHANDRA SINGH
Maharaja of Mannipur

Sd/
V.P. Menon
Advisor to the Government
of India

Sd/
SRIPRAKASA
(Governor of Assam)
Shillong, September 21, 1949

(Source: Aribam Brajakumar Sharma (ed), *Influx of Migrants into Manipur*, (Imphal: UCM, 2005) pp. 158-163.

APPENDIX IV

THE ARMED FORCES (SPECIAL POWERS) ACT, 1958

Act 28 of 1958, 11th September, 1958

An Act to enable certain special powers to be conferred upon members of the armed forces in disturbed areas in the State of [1][Arunachal Pradesh, Assam, Manipur, Meghalaya, Mizoram, Nagaland and Tripura].

Be it enacted by Parliament in the Ninth Year of the Republic of India as follows:

1. Short Title and Extent – (1) This Act may be called[2] [The Armed Forces (Special Powers) Act, 1958].

   [3][(2) It extends to the whole of the State of [4][Arunachal Pradesh, Assam, Manipur, Meghalaya, Mizoram, Nagaland and Tripura].

2. Definitions – In this Act, unless the context otherwise requires:

   (a) "armed forces" means the Military forces and the air forces operating as land forces, and includes any other armed forces of the Union so operating;

   (b) "disturbed area" means an area which is for the time being declared by notification under section 3, to be a disturbed area;

   (c) all other words and expressions used herein, but not defined and defined in the Air Force Act, 1950 (45 of 1950), or the Army Act, 1950 (46 of 1950) shall have meanings respectively assigned to them in those Acts.

[3][3. Power to Declare Areas to be Disturbed Areas – If, in relation to any State or Union territory of which the Act extends, the Governor of that State or the Administrator

of that Union territory or the Central Government, in either case, if of the opinion that the whole or any part of such State or Union territory, as the case may be, is in such a disturbed or dangerous condition that the use of armed forces in aid of the civil powers is necessary, the Governor of that State or the Administrator of that Union territory or the Central Government, as the case may be, may, by notification in the Official Gazette, declare the whole or such part of such State or Union territory to be a disturbed area].

4. Special Power of the Armed Forces – Any commissioned officer, warrant officer, non commissioned officer or any other person of equivalent rank in the armed forces may, in a disturbed area-

   (a) if he is of opinion that it is necessary so to do for the maintenance of Public order, after giving such due warning as he may consider necessary, fire upon or otherwise use force, even to causing of death, against any person who is acting in contravention of any law or order for the time being in force in the disturbed area prohibiting the assembly of five or more persons or the carrying of weapons or of things capable of being used as weapons or of fire-arms, ammunition or explosive substances;

   (b) if he is of opinion that it is necessary so to do, destroy any arms dump, prepared or fortified position or shelter from which armed attacks are made or are likely to be made or are attempted to be made, or any structure used as a training camp for armed volunteers or utilised as a hide-out by armed gangs or absconders wanted for any offence;

   (c) arrest, without warrant, any person who has committed a cognizable offence or against whom a reasonable suspicion exists that he has committed or is about to commit a cognizable offence and may use such force as may be necessary to effect the arrest;

(d) enter and search without warrant any premises to make any such arrest as aforesaid or to recover any person believed to be wrongfully restrained or confined or any property reasonably suspected to be stolen property or any arms, ammunition or explosive substances believed to be unlawfully kept in such premises and may for that purpose use such force as may be necessary.

5. Arrested Persons to be made over to the Police – Any person arrested and taken into custody under this Act shall be made over to the officer-in-charge of the nearest police station with the least possible delay, together with a report of the circumstances occasioning the arrest.

6. Protection to Persons acting under Act – No persecution, suit or other legal proceeding shall be instituted, except with the previous sanction of the Central Government, against any person in respect of anything done or purported to be done in exercise of the powers conferred by this Act.

7. Repeal and Saving – [Repealed by Amending and Repealing Act, 1960 (58 of 1960), First Schedule, sec. 2 (26-12-1960)]

1. Subs. By Act 69 of 1986, sec. 43, for "Assam, Manipur, Meghalaya, Mizoram, Nagaland and Tripura and the Union Territory of Arunachal Pradesh" (w.e.f. 20-2-1987).

2. Subs. By Act 7 of 1972, sec. 3, for "the Armed Forces (Assam and Manipur) Special Powers Act., 1958" (w.e.f. 5-4-1972)

3. Subs. By Act 7 of 1972, sec. 4 (w.e.f. 5-4-1972)

4 .Subs. By Act 69 of 1986, sec. 43, for "Assam, Manipur, Meghalaya, Mizoram, Nagaland and Tripura and the Union territory of Arunachal Pradesh" (w.e.f. 20-2-1987).

APPENDIX V

9TH ASSEMBLY ELECTIONS, 2007, RESULTS

Constituency	Winner	Party	Nearest rival	Party
1.Khundrakpam	Thokchom Navakumar Singh	NCP	Laishram Premchandra Singh	CPI
2. Heingang	Nongthombam Biren	Congress	Mutum Babita Devi	MPP
3. Khurai	Dr. Ngairangbam Bijoy Singh	MPP	N. Bihari Singh	Congress
4. Khetrigao	Thangjam Nandakishor Singh	NCP	Mohd. Amin Shah	Congress
5. Thangju	Bijoy Koijam	Congress	Thokchom Ajit	IND
6.Keirao	Alauddin Khan	Congress	Karan Thamarjit Singh	MSCP
7. Andro	Thounaojam Shyamkumar	MPP	Salam Chandra Singh	Congress
8.Lamlai	Pheiroijam Parijat	CPI	K. Biren Singh	Congress
9. Thangmeiband	Radhabinod Koijam	NCP	Jyotin Waikhom	Congress
10. Uripok	Laisharm Nandakumar Singh	Congress	P. Achou Singh	MPP
11. Sagolband	Dr. Khwairakpam Loken Singh	Congress	Soram Natum Singh	RJD

(Contd...)

Constituency	*Winner*	*Party*	*Nearest rival*	*Party*
12.Keishamthong	L. Jayantakumar Singh	Congress	Laisom Ibomcha	MPP
13.Singjamei	I. Hemochanda Singh	Congress	Sapam Tiken Singh	MPP
14.Yaiskul	Elangbam Kunjeswar Singh	Congress	Raj Kumar Dorendra Singh	MPP
15. Wanghei	Yumkham Erabot Singh	Congress	Amouban Rajen	MPP
16.Sekmai (SC)	Dr. Heikham Borajao	CPI	Ninthoujam Biren	Congress
17. Lamsang	Wangkheimayum Brajabidhu	Congress	S. Rajen Singh	MPP
18.Konthoujam	Dr. Sapam Budhichadra Singh	Congress	K. Sarat Singh	NPP
19. Patsoi	Sapam Kunjakeswor Singh	Ind	Dr. Chandramani Singh	MPP
20.Langthabal	Okram Bijoy Singh	MPP	Rebika Naorem	NCP
21.Naoriya Pakhanglakpa	R.K. Anand	MPP	K. Rojenkumar Singh	RJD
22.Wangoi	Salam Bijoy Singh	NCP	W. Nipamacha Singh	RJD
23.Mayang Imphal	Dr. Khumujam Ratan Kumar Singh	Congress	Maulan Abdus Salam	NCP

(Contd...)

Constituency	Winner	Party	Nearest rival	Party
24.Nambol	Nameirakpam Loken Singh	Congress	Tjounaojam Chaoba	MPP
25.Oinam	Irengbam Ibohalbi	MPP	L. Radhakishore	Congress
26.Bishenpur	Konthoujam Govindas	Congress	N. Sanajaoba	MPP
27.Moirang	M. Manindra	Congress	Salam Gopal Singh	MPP
28. Thanga	Tongbram Mangibabu Singh	Congress	H. Manisan Singh	MPP
29. Kumbi	Ningthoujam Mangi	CPI	Sanasam Biren Singh	Congress
30. Linong	Helaluddin Khan	RJD	Dr. Maniruddin Shaikh	Congress
31. Thoubal	Okram Ibobi Singh	Congress	L. Thomba Singh	MPP
32. Wangkhem	K. Meghachandra Singh	Congress	Dr. Nimaichandra Luwang	MPP
33. Heirok	M. Okendro	Congress	N. Savakiran Singh	MPP
34. Wangjing Tentha	Moirangthem Hemanta Singh	Congress	Moirangthem Nara Singh	CPI
35. Khangabok	Okram Ibobi Singh	Congress	Laishram Jatra Singh	MPP

(Contd...)

Constituency	Winner	Party	Nearest rival	Party
36. Wabgai	Dr. Usham Deben Singh	CPI	M. Manihar Singh	MSCP
37. Kakching	Yengkhom Surendra Singh	Congress	Thokchom Tomba	CPI
38. Hiyanglam	Elangbam Dwijamani Singh	Congress	Maibam Kunjo Singh	NCP
39. Sugnoo	Kangujam Ranjit Singh	Congress	M. Binod (Chaoba)	MPP
40. Jiribam	Thoudam Debendra	Congress	A. Biren	NCP
41. Chandel (ST)	Thangkholun Haokip	RJD	L. Benjamin	Ind
42. Tengnoupal (ST)	W. Morung Makunga	Ind	Chungsei	RJD
43. Phungyar (ST)	K. Waungnaoshang	Ind	Victor Keishing	Congress
44. Ukhrul (ST)	Danny Shaiza	Ind	A.S. Arthur	Congress
45. Chingai (ST)	Dr. Khashim Ruiyah	Ind	A. Aza	Congress
46. Saikul (ST)	Doukhomang Khongsai	NCP	Chungkhokai Doungel	Congress
47. Karong (ST)	D.D. Thaishi	Congress	L. Jonathan	Ind
48. Mao (ST)	M. Thohrii	Ind	W. Joram	Ind

(Contd...)

Constituency	Winner	Party	Nearest rival	Party
49.Tadubi (ST)	K. Raina	Ind	N. Kayisii	Ind
50. Kangpokpi	Thangminlen Kipgen	NPP	Kishor Thapa	Ind
51. Saitu (ST)	Haokholet Kipgen	Ind	Ngamthang Haokip	Congress
52. Tamei (ST)	Awangbow Newmei	Ind	Z. Mangaibou	Congress
53.Tamenglong (ST)	Khangthuanang Panmei	Ind	Samuel Jendai	Ind
54.Nungba (ST)	Gaikhangam	Congress	Gangmumei Kamei	Ind
55.Tipaimukh (ST)	Ngursanglur	RJD	Dr. Chaltonlien Amo	Congress
56. Thanlon (ST)	V. Hangkanlian	NPP	Zabiaksang	BJP
57. Henglep (ST)	T. Manga Vaiphei	Congress	T. Thangjalam Haokip	LJP
58. Churachand-pur (ST)	Phungzathang Tonsing	Congress	V. Langkhanpau Guite	NPP
59. Saikot (ST)	T.N. Haokip	Congress	Lalthanlien	NCP
60.Singhat (ST)	T. Hangkhanpao	NPP	Thangso Baite	Congress

Source: Election Commission of India

BIBLIOGRAPHY

Ahmed, Abu Nasar Saied *et. al., Election Politics in Assam* (New Delhi: Akansha Publishing House, 2006).

Allen, B.C.: *Gazetteer of Naga Hills and Manipur,* First Published in 1905 (New Delhi: Mittal Pulications, 2002).

Bhagat, Oinam and A. Bimal Akoijam, "Manipur: Assesmbly Election: Trends and Issues", *Economic and Political Weekly,* February, 9, 2002, pp. 519-524.

Brass, Paul, "Coalition Politics in North India", *American Politicl Science Review,* Vol, 62, No. 4 December, 1968, pp. 1174-1191.

Campbell, Angus, *et al., Elections and Political Order* (New York: John Wiley and Sons, 1968).

Chakrabarty, Bidyut, *Forging Power: Coalition Politics in India* (New Delhi: Oxford University Press, 2006).

Chanu, *Insurgency Movement in Manipur,* Working Paper Series 09 (Guwahati: OKDISCD, 2004).

Chishti, S.M.A.W., *Kuki Uprising in Manipur: 1917-1920* (Guwahati: Omson, 2004).

Chishti, S.M.A.W., *Political Development in Manipur: 1919-1949* (New Delhi: Kalpaz, 2005).

Crawford, C.G., *Administrative Report, Manipur State,* Volume I-V (Imphal: State Printing Press, 1923-1927).

Devi Kh, Elizabeth, "Political Instability in Manipur: Nature and Causes", an unpublished working paper (Guwahati: OKDISCD, 2003).

Davies, Oliver *et al.*, "An expository development of a mathematical model of the electoral process", *American Political Science Review,* Vol. 64, No. 2, 1970, pp. 426-428

Dena, Lal (ed), *History of Modern Manipur (1826-1949)* (New Delhi: Orbit Publishers, 1991).

Devi, Kh. Sarojini, *British Political Agency in Manipur 1835-1947* (Imphal: Linthoi Publications, 2005).

Devi, P. Binodini, *Tribal Land System of Manipur* (New Delhi: Akansha Publishing House, 2006).

Dutta, Anuradha and Ratna Bhuyan, *Genesis of Peace and Conflict in Northeast India,* Vol. I and II (New Delhi: Akansha Publishing House, 2007).

Gangte, Tangkhomang, S., *The Kukis of Manipur: A Historical Analysis* (New Delhi: Gyan Publishing House, 2003).

Ganguly, Jalad Baran, *An Economic History of North East India: 1926-1947* (New Delhi: Akansha Publishing House, 2006).

Gopalakrishnan, R. and C.J. Thomas (eds), *Conflicts to Reconstruction: Some Observations on Nagaland and Manipur* (New Delhi: Regency Publications, 2005).

Indrakumar, Haobam, *Basic Dimension of Indentity and Integration: A Critical Appraisal of Meetei Perspective* (Imphal: Leisem Laisuthoukaikol, 2002).

Johnstone, Sir James, *Manipur and the Naga Hills* (New Delhi: Gyan Publications, 2002).

Kabui, Gangmumei, *History of Manipur* (New Delhi: National Publishing House, 2003).

Kabui, Gangmumei, "Insurgency in Manipur Valley" in B.L. Abbi (ed), *North East Region: Problem and Prospects of Development* (Chandigarh: Centre for Research in Rural and Industrial Development, 1984), pp. 233-234.

Kamei, Gangmumei, *On History and Historiography of Manipur* (New Delhi: Akansha Publishing House, 2006).

Kashyap, Subhash C., *The Politics of Defection: A Study of State Politics in India* (New Delhi: Continental Publishing House, 1969).

Kshetri, Rajendra, *District Councils in Manipur: Formation and Functioning* (New Delhi: Akansha Publishing House, 2006).

Marwah, Ved, *Uncivil Wars: Pathology of Terrorism in India* (New Delhi: Harper and Collins, 1995).

Marwah, Ved, "India's Internal Security Challenges", *Strategic Analysis,* Vol. 27, No. 4, October-December, 2003, pp. 503-515.

Nepram, Binalakshmi, *South Asia's Fractured Frontier* (New Delhi: Mittal Publications, 2002).

Pakem, B., *Coalition Political in North-East India* (New Delhi: Regency Publications, 1999).

Palmer, Norman D., "Fourth General Election", *Asian Survey,* Vol. 7, No. 5, May 1967, pp. 275-291.

Palmer, Norman D., "Elections and the Political System in India: The State Assembly Elections and After", *Pacific Affaris,* Vol. 45, No. 4, Winter 1972-73, pp. 535-555.

Pemberton, R. Boileau, *The Eastern Frontier of India,* reprint (New Delhi: Mittal Publications, 2000).

Rabinowitz, G and S.E. Macdonald, "A directional theory issue voting", *American Political Science Review,* Vol. 83, No. 1, 1989, pp. 93-121.

Roy, Ramashray, *et al., Northeast India: Development,*

Communalism and Insurgency (New Delhi: Anshah Publishing House, 2007).

Sanajaoba, N. (ed), *Manipur: A British Anthology,* Vol. 1 (New Delhi: Akansha Publishing House, 2003).

Sandham, Oken Jeet, "Who Rules Manipur Streets?," manipurline.com, September, 30, 2005.

Sanjenbam, Vedaja, *Manipur: Geogrpahy and Regional Development* (New Delhi: Rajesh Publication, 1998).

Sharma, Aribam Brajakumar (ed), *Influx of Migrants into Manipur: A Threat to the Indigenous Ethnic People* (Imphal: United Committee Manipur, 2005).

Singh, Mahendra, Prasad, and Anil Misra (eds), *Coalition Politics in India and Prospects* (New Delhi: Manohar, 2004).

Singh, Naorem Joy Kumar, *Colonialism to Democracy: A History of Manipur 1819-1972* (Guwahati: Spectrum, 2002).

Singh, N. Joy Kumar, *Social Movements in Manipur* (New Delhi: Mittal, 2005).

Singh, Naorem Joykumar, *Federal Party of Manipur: 1993-2000 AD* (New Delhi: Akansha Publishing House, 2006).

Singh, N. Mohendra (ed), *Development Experience in Manipur* (Imphal: Institute of Development Studies, 2002).

Singh, O. Kulabidhu, *Sharmila: A Mission for Peace* (Imphal: Oinam Ongbi Gulapmachu Devi, 2006).

Stroke, Donald E., "Spatial Models of Party Competition", *American Political Science Review,* Vol. 57, No. 1, 1963, pp. 368-377.

Thomas, C.J. *et al., Constraints of Development in Manipur* (New Delhi: Regency Publications, 2001).

United Committee, *Manipur, The Greater Autonomy of Manipur: A Demand of the People of Manipur* (Imphal: June 2003).

Verghese, B.G., *India's Northeast Resurgent: Ethnicity, Insurgency, Governance, Development* (New Delhi: Konark Publishers, 1996).

Newspapers:

Telegraph
Imphal Free Press
Sentinel
Sangai Express
Paknaphyam
Thoudang

INDEX